THE HEART OF A SON

Book 1 in the Kingdom Life Focus Series

THE HEART OF A SON

SERVING WELL IN GOD'S KINGDOM

FOREWORD BY DR. MARK KAUFFMAN

DR. ED TUROSE

Volant, Pennsylvania

THE HEART OF A SON

© 2022 Dr. Ed Turose. All Rights Reserved.

This book is protected by the copyright laws of the United States of America. This book may not be copied or reprinted for commercial gain or profit. The use of short quotations is permitted. Permission will be granted upon request. The author guarantees all contents are original and do not infringe upon the legal rights of any other person or work.

Printed in the USA

ISBN (print): 978-0-9980161-2-2

ISBN (ePUB): 978-0-9980161-3-9

Library of Congress Control Number (LCCN): 2022916250

Edited by Theresa Burnworth

Cover Design by Wendy K. Walters

Prepared for Publication by www.palmtreeproductions.com

Published by Ed Turose—Volant, PA

Scripture marked AMP has been taken from the Amplified Bible. Copyright © 2015 by The Lockman Foundation, La Habra, CA. Used by permission. www.lockman.org.

Scripture marked AMPC has been taken from the Amplified Bible Classic Edition. Copyright © 1954, 1958, 1962, 1964, 1965, 1987 by The Lockman Foundation, La Habra, CA. Used by permission. www.lockman.org

Scripture marked KJV has been taken from the King James Version of the Bible and is in the public domain.

Scripture marked NKJV has been taken from the New King James Version®. Copyright © 1982 by Thomas Nelson. Used by permission. All rights reserved.

Scripture marked NIV has been taken from THE HOLY BIBLE, NEW INTERNATIONAL VERSION®, NIV® Copyright © 1973, 1978, 1984, 2011 by Biblica, Inc.® Used by permission. All rights reserved worldwide.

Scripture marked TPT has been taken from The Passion Translation®. Copyright © 2017, 2018, 2020 by Passion & Fire Ministries, Inc. Used by permission. All rights reserved. ThePassionTranslation.com.

To contact the author:
www.FocusLifeInstitute.com

THE HEART OF A SON

PRAISE FOR THE HEART OF A SON

It has been with great honor for the past 48 years to have walked this life with my husband. He has always been a man after God's heart. I've watched and experienced in every situation we've encountered how he sought counsel and obeyed the voice of God through the still, small voice, and honored those he's been submitted to in the church and in business. He has been tenacious in his pursuit to do all things God's way through the spirit of wisdom and revelation. This revelation of *The Heart of a Son* is imperative for the church today. An apostle cannot move the Kingdom of God forward without sons, and they must have his heart for the vision. Our assignment as sons is to carry the government on our shoulders. Jesus, the perfect Son, revealed His Father's heart in everything He did. Let us do the same as Dr. Ed has shown us practically in this book on how to be a son.

CINDY TUROSE
Wife, Jubilee Ministries Lead Intercessor

There comes a time in a person's life that they must begin to walk out what they have learned. The Jewish saying is that you haven't truly heard a thing until you do it. We are filled with revelation in this day, but it is not enough to hear it, we must live it. *The Heart of a Son* is spiritual yet practical. Through many actual life experiences, Dr. Ed teaches us how to live out this Word and live the life of a true son! I highly recommend this book for all—those who are just starting out on their journey and also those who have been on the journey for years! Keep this in your library. You will read it over and over!

DR. JILL KAUFFMAN, M.Div, D.Div.
Jubilee Ministries International

THE HEART OF A SON

I want to congratulate Dr. Ed Turose on producing a quintessential, logical, and pragmatic book for equipping sons for God and His Kingdom. This book provides step-by-step guidelines for discovering, developing, and demonstrating your God-given purpose and potential. Both spiritual fathers and sons will benefit greatly if the instructions in this book are followed systematically and truthfully.

DR VINCENT G. VALENTYN
B.Div (RSA) B.BA (UK) M.Div Cum Laude (USA) Ph.D. Honoris Causa (USA)
Kingdom Lifestyle Ministries International, Cape Town, South Africa

There's an old saying, "When you read a good book, you should be able to hear the voice of the author." I hear Ed's voice loud and clear in this fabulous book. I've known Ed and his family for many years, and his passion to be a faithful son is evident in every part of his life in Christ. Sonship involves servanthood at the highest level, being willing to pour water on the hands of a father, being willing to take care of another man's field, and as Jesus said, "If you've seen Me, you've seen the Father!" As sons, we must have a father in the faith that we can emulate and honor and receive from to help us move into our role as fathers in God's Kingdom! This is a book that reveals the Father's heart that so many are crying out for in this day!

BISHOP BART PIERCE
Rock City Church, Baltimore, Maryland

For nearly two decades, I had the honor of standing with Dr. Ed Turose as we battled spiritually for the lives of his son and mine. During that time, I discovered in him what I have missed seeing in many others—the understanding of how fathers and sons relate, both naturally and spiritually, and how a father is uniquely suited to draw the best out of a son. As I have watched Ed draw the best out of his son, and encourage me

THE HEART OF A SON

to do so with my own, I have also watched as he has allowed God to draw the best out of him as a son. He has demonstrated true sonship before the Father, and also with the fathering voices that God has woven into his life. If Dr. Turose's instruction on focus depicts his ministry, his teaching on sonship depicts his life! This book is a must-read if you want to discover how relating to God as a son will draw out the best in your life!

APOSTLE TIMOTHY BYLER, DRE, Relatable Leadership
CEO-Connection Ministry Network, Hinesville, Georgia

In his book, *The Heart of a Son*, Dr. Ed Turose shares his journey to pursue his purpose at the highest level of excellence and honor in a corporate Fortune 100 company and in the church. I love the six points he revisits from his first book, *The HEROES Effect*: Honor, Excellence, Responsibility, Order, Expectation, and Servanthood. The truths that he shares bring life and success to every environment. You will be challenged to a path of truth that will give breakthroughs.

Dr. Ed Turose clarifies truths that help us keep our focus. I love his practical points that we instinctively know, but sometimes lose focus in the heat of the battle. My wife's favorite part of the book covers the secret of victory. Only those who submit to authority as a son will ever carry authority. Jesus demonstrated this truth under Father God for all of us to gain revelation on the key to authority. She has witnessed Dr. Ed Turose's submissive heart and powerful authority within Jubilee Ministries. All of us must step up in our sonship to attain heaven's best for our life on earth. Shift your expectation, honor the authority Father God has placed in your life, and live a dream.

DR. DALE L MAST, LUANNE L MAST
Senior Pastors, International Speakers
Authors of *And David Perceived He Was King, Two Sons and A Father, The Throne of David, Shattering the Limitations of Pain, God,* and *I Feel Like Cinderella!*

THE HEART OF A SON

In his new book, *The Heart of The Son,* Dr. Turose has captured the essence of sonship in the Kingdom of God. In chapter one, he takes us right to the most important thing any son of God can do—spend quality time in the presence of our Heavenly Father and hear His voice. Dr. Turose combines Scripture, life experiences, and prophetic words that lead us into a deeper understanding of the processes of God. He speaks to us of our relationship with our earthly father, our spiritual father, and our Heavenly Father. This book reminds us that sons are purposed for assignment and are to operate in the highest levels of honor and excellence. We must align ourselves with our spiritual fathers to fulfill vision and advance the Kingdom of God in the earth. This book is a must-read for anyone who desires to move forward in service to our King Jesus.

PASTOR TONY FLOWERS
Jubilee Ministries International

Ed Turose is a modern-day Abraham. Everything about his life exhibits that he is a son of the Covenant. I grew up in the faith, rooted and grounded in the Word, and walking the talk, but before I met Ed Turose, I did not truly understand what being "blessed to be a blessing" meant. He is a walking word everywhere he goes—a living epistle not written by hands. He models what he communicates, and *The Heart of a Son* is just that, the heart of Ed Turose written down. In these pages, you will glimpse the man I have come to love, respect, and trust as a servant, priest, and king. Take his words to heart. If you apply them, you cannot help but level up.

WENDY K. WALTERS
Entrepreneur, Master Coach, Founder of The Favor Foundation

THE HEART OF A SON

DEDICATION

*This book is dedicated to the enlightening power
of the Holy Spirit who guides and directs our pathway
and brings us into our assignment, purpose, and destiny to
advance the Kingdom of God.*

*My wife, Cindy—my intercessor, my strength
during good and hard times, who is always
willing to go higher in God, and follows the
leading of the Holy Spirit to enjoy the
journey of the Kingdom.*

*My children, Theresa and Dan—who believed in their parents
to lead them to their destinies and who
have followed God fully in their lives.*

*To our three beautiful grandchildren—Joel,
Seth, and Elia who serve and love God, providing a legacy of
our family to advance the Kingdom of God.*

*To my spiritual father and mother—Apostle Mark
and Apostle Jill Kauffman because your love,
counsel, direction, and support have led us into
fulfilling our purpose and destiny.
We love you with our life!*

THE HEART OF A SON

THE HEART OF A SON

CONTENTS

FOREWORD BY DR. MARK KAUFFMAN	1
INTRODUCTION **MY PERSPECTIVE ON BEING A SON**	5
CHAPTER ONE **PRESENCE OF SONS**	11
CHAPTER TWO **PURPOSE OF SONS**	25
CHAPTER THREE **PREPARATION OF SONS**	35
CHAPTER FOUR **PERFECTION OF SONS**	47
CHAPTER FIVE **POSITION OF SONS**	69
CHAPTER SIX **PROCESS OF SONS**	79
CHAPTER SEVEN **PROPHETIC OF SONS**	97
CHAPTER EIGHT **PLAN OF SONS**	105
CHAPTER NINE **PRINCIPLES OF SONS**	111
CHAPTER TEN **PROTOCOL OF SONS**	121
SUMMARY **POSITIVE IMPACT OF SONS**	133
APPENDIX	139

THE HEART OF A SON

FOREWORD BY DR. MARK KAUFFMAN

In this present season, God is administrating His Kingdom through a wineskin called fathers and sons (male and female). In ages gone by, this has been God's divine order for fulfilling His purposes trans-generationally. It is God's pattern for building His holy nation in the earth. Presently the church is in transition. We are moving from the Church Age into the Apostolic Father-Son Kingdom Age. Apostolic fathers are emerging in this hour to put vision into the sons of God who will transform the planet with the culture of heaven.

The call of God in this present hour is for the church to upgrade by finding their spiritual father assigned to their life. Like Jesus who left Galilee (circles) and went to the Jordan (descender), we must also leave our Galilee, the place where religion takes us in circles. The time has come to break away and find our John the Baptist (spiritual father) at the Jordan, where we can humble ourselves and submit to true spiritual authority. Every man and woman of God who wants to fulfill their divine destiny must find a spiritual father who will baptize them and immerse them in the water of God's present-day truths, so they can proceed to their destiny and live life under an open heaven.

Jesus is the pattern Son for this divine order. Remember, only when Jesus submitted to this divine order did the heavens open up to Him. This realm was opened for Jesus during His entire three-and-a-half-year ministry. It is within this open heaven that Father God takes the limitations off the miracles we need. In an open heaven, God's treasury

THE HEART OF A SON

and armory will be opened up for you. When His treasuries open, the resources you need to fulfill your destiny will come looking for you.

As a result of these father-son relationships, Father God is building a family. The Hebrew root meaning of family is "Father's house." Every true father in the earth travails in birth until Christ is formed within the sons of God. God started with the family in Genesis, and in these end times, He will restore His apostolic family back in the earth. Every true spiritual father has a strong sense for family. The true heart of apostolic fathers is to build God's family in the planet.

Without this apostolic order, there is no visitation of the Lord in the land. As these apostolic families are restored in the earth, it becomes the channel to release the desire of heaven upon the earth, whereby the Lord will visit the land again and heal the nations. And in this new day, Jesus will have a bride, the Holy Ghost will have a temple, and the Father will have a family.

Success without successors is failure in disguise. Abraham, who raised up sons as successors, is a beautiful model of this father-son paradigm that we can use to build God's Kingdom in the earth. According to this Genesis 14:14-15 model we see that:

- His sons were equipped
- His sons were trained
- His sons served in the house
- His sons receive the covenant blessings of the house
- His sons ran with him
- His sons stood with him in the night seasons
- His sons received their inheritance

INTRODUCTION

Dr. Ed Turose's new book, *The Heart of a Son*, takes us on a journey of the maturation process of a son of God. This is a handbook and a manual that is long overdue. Previously many books have been written on how to be a father to spiritual sons and daughters, but finally, a book on how to live like a son in the Kingdom of God! Dr. Ed's life experiences are a deep revelation of how the Holy Spirit apprehends, develops, and deploys His chosen sons.

Dr. Turose has modeled within the local church, his home, and in the marketplace the spirit of sonship. His gift cluster, good work ethics, professionalism, and marketability are the lesser qualifications that are required for a son of God and great leadership. The much weightier qualification is his distinct call to serve, his excellent spirit, his generous heart, and the spirit of honor that rests on his life. Dr. Ed not only teaches and preaches sonship, he lives it! It has been my great honor to serve him and his family, preparing them for their great destiny that lies ahead.

I will promote this book everywhere I go and will encourage fivefold leaders to use this book as a training manual for their followers. This book has been incredibly written, and not only carries my endorsement, but my great desire for it to be a roadmap for each and every one who reads it into sonship and into the fulfillment of their destinies in Christ.

As you read this masterpiece and reread it again, it will empower you, equip you, and thrust you into a new dimension of God's glory for your life! Read it. Reread it. Meditate on it. Believe it. Live it. Be it!

DR. MARK KAUFFMAN

Senior Pastor Jubilee Ministries International
CEO Butz Flowers and Gifts
Founder Apostolic Congress of Pennsylvania
Founder Christian Chamber of Commerce of PA
Lead Apostle International Network of Kingdom Leaders

THE HEART OF A SON

SUCCESS WITHOUT
SUCCESSORS IS FAILURE
IN DISGUISE.

DR. MARK KAUFFMAN

INTRODUCTION
MY PERSPECTIVE ON BEING A SON

*For the earnest expectation of the creature
waiteth for the manifestation of the sons of God.
For we know that the whole creation groaneth
and travaileth in pain together until now.*
ROMANS 8:19, 22 KJV

It's time for the manifestations of the sons of God! God wants to equip and train you as a true son of God (male and female) to reign as a king in life. By understanding how to operate as a military might, we advance His Kingdom in the earth! God has prophetically spoken to me to rally the troops to focus on how to have the heart of a true son to serve the apostles that are being established in this age that will impact and influence culture to manifest the glory of God in the earth.

*There is neither Jew nor Greek, there is neither
bond nor free, there is neither male nor
female: for ye are all one in Christ Jesus.*
GALATIANS 3:28 KJV

THE HEART OF A SON

I am talking to those who want to fulfill the cry of creation! All creation is groaning for the sons, both male, and female, of God to take their place to redeem society by the reformation and restoration of the Kingdom of God in the earth.

The culture we live in today is broken, and we are witnessing a cultural war! The worldly system is crumbling, and they lack the answers and solutions to fix it. Darkness and gross darkness (Isaiah 60:2) are upon the land, and we have entered the beginning of sorrows (Matthew 24:8). This is not good news for those still living by the worldly system, and especially for Kingdom believers who need to reject that system (Revelation 18:4) and enter the marvelous light of the Kingdom of God.

As a leader in the church for over 40 years, I have been schooled by the Holy Spirit on how to serve Father God and His set man and woman that He has placed over me. I have learned how to help fulfill the local, corporate vision along with my calling and assignment to advance God's Kingdom. It's time for the sons of God to arise!

I have had many discussions with apostles and pastors, and they all agree that they struggle to equip and train up sons in their network or churches—men and women to help fulfill the vision that God has given them over a specific region or territory. In fact, many have told me that no one has ever written a book from the position of a son to explain how true sons honor and serve their spiritual father and mother.

God always uses a man or woman to lead the fulfillment of His promises over a city or region. By submitting and staying under the covering of a spiritual father, sons walk in protection and receive the grace to fulfill the vision God has given the spiritual covering for their territory. Furthermore, God's grace also extends to you personally to fulfill your life's assignment and purpose alongside your spiritual father and mother.

MY PERSPECTIVE ON BEING A SON

And if ye have not been faithful in that which is another man's, who shall give you that which is your own?
LUKE 16:12 KJV

This has been a key verse for the past 40 years to me. My wife and I have personally served another man's vision and continue to do so to fulfill the corporate vision. Our responsibility is to help generations at an early age to know and understand their assignment as a son of God to reveal His Kingdom. It is time that the mature sons arise, step into their roles, and positively change our culture to let the light and the glory of the Kingdom shine (Isaiah 60:1).

My passion is to advance the Kingdom of God and change generations with the revelation, experiences, and practical tools that God has so graciously provided for me in my life through the Focus Life Institute (www.focuslifeinstitute.com). I must equip and train the next generations to quickly enter their sphere of influence so they may fulfill their assignments and destinies to transform the world culture into a Kingdom culture where all God's enemies become His footstool (see Psalm 110:1).

This book is based on my personal experiences that can help you understand how to walk in your God-given assignment and function as a son to serve your set man or woman in a Kingdom church. The only way your spirit man will be filled and full is when you are doing the will of your Father! This is why after 37 years as a Fortune 100 manager for Unilever and the Coca-Cola Company, I retired early to equip and train generations in both practical and personal development in the advancement of the Kingdom of God. I pray that you will glean from my experiences and personal testimonies in these pages.

At the end of each chapter, please take time to read and answer the prompts. As you review these principles and patterns, take time in your

THE HEART OF A SON

intimate, focused environment, your quiet place, and allow the Holy Spirit to teach you what you need to do to inherit your possession and walk in the POWER of the Kingdom.

> *"Our purpose is to be intimate with Him,*
> *and our destiny is to manifest Him."*
> DR. MARK KAUFFMAN

The Heart of a Son, a Kingdom Focus Life book, consists of the areas you need to FOCUS on to mature in your calling and assignment from a Kingdom perspective. To daily walk in the power of God and manifest Him, you must understand how to consistently pursue His presence, put on His new nature created in the image of God, and ascend to the higher life in Christ.

> *But you did not so learn Christ! Assuming that you have really heard Him and been taught by Him, as [all] Truth is in Jesus [embodied and personified in Him], Strip yourselves of your former nature [put off and discard your old unrenewed self] which characterized your previous manner of life and becomes corrupt through lusts and desires that spring from delusion; And be constantly renewed in the spirit of your mind [having a fresh mental and spiritual attitude], And put on the new nature (the regenerate self) created in God's image, [Godlike] in true righteousness and holiness.*
> EPHESIANS 4:20-24 AMPC

The highest calling we have is to be transformed and conformed to the image and likeness of Jesus Christ and to advance His Kingdom. My prayer is that you will be able to fully enter into this Father Son Kingdom

MY PERSPECTIVE ON BEING A SON

Age, maturing as sons of God to fulfill His agenda on the earth and see His glory manifest through your obedience as a son!

Thou shalt increase my greatness, and
comfort me on every side.
PSALM 71:21 KJV

THE HEART OF A SON

IT'S TIME FOR YOUR MOMENT TO STEP INTO GREATNESS AND BE A SON!

CHAPTER ONE
PRESENCE OF SONS

God's presence is the most vital element in your role as a son. Jesus, the prime example, demonstrated how He loved to be in the presence of His Father. The Father's heart is toward a son who comes into the quiet place, alone with His Father in a focused environment, to hear His Father's voice and obey what he hears. Yes, our life has a purpose, but His presence must be first so we can hear His voice to truly fulfill our corporate and individual assignments.

My spiritual father and mother, Drs. Mark and Jill Kauffman, have created a mandate for our church family that we declare corporately, and one sentence from it reads, "Our purpose is to be intimate with the Lord, and our destiny is to manifest Him in the earth!" Think about that! Intimacy with God leads to purpose and destiny. David's greatest desire was to be in the Lord's presence. In fact, he was the only one we read about in Scripture who had a heart after God (Acts 13:22). For those reasons, he was chosen for greatness.

THE HEART OF A SON

David declared from this famous passage:

> *One thing have I desired of the Lord, that will I seek after; that I may dwell in the house of the Lord all the days of my life, to behold the beauty of the Lord, and to enquire in His temple.*
> PSALM 27:4 KJV

Between 1977 when I graduated college, until August 1988, I attended a church that was not teaching present-day truth. After the Holy Spirit revealed this to us, we obeyed Him and relocated to a different church in a nearby town. We received multiple prophetic words that confirmed this was to be our church, and my entire family was filled with the Holy Ghost in this place. Thus began our Kingdom journey.

After a year in this church, I was able to gain an understanding of the culture of this new house of God. I learned more about what it meant to submit to my spiritual father at the time, and God raised me up in leadership. However, there was only one way I was going to sustain my schedule with family, work, and church. I was managing a $75 million territory for my job that included traveling 2-3 days a week. My wife and I began leading a weekly house group meeting in our home. It grew to over 50 adults and 20 children.

Meanwhile, I was singing on the worship team in 2 services each Sunday, attending weekly prayer meetings, and balancing it all with family time with my wife and two children. To manage such a full schedule, I needed His presence! I received this timely, prophetic word during

PRESENCE OF SONS

those years from a great woman of God, Fuchsia Pickett, that started my understanding of cultivating intimacy with the Lord.

I received this word by Fuchsia Pickett on November 9, 1992:

> *You have been one that has been saying, "I want the Teacher to teach me the Book." You say, "I want to be able to hear what He said, not what somebody else said." You have cried out to want to know revelation; well, I have news for you. My Father says that Ephesians, the first chapter beginning to the 15th verse, is going to be yours. He is going to grant unto you not a word of wisdom, not a word of knowledge, but the Spirit of Wisdom and the Spirit of Knowledge. The Spirit of Wisdom and the Spirit of Knowledge. And the Teacher is on duty. Don't stay out of the classroom, don't stay out of the classroom—the classroom is inside of you! Go in, read that Book, and have Him teach it to you. Cause He said, "There is open to you a Spirit of Wisdom, not just a word." The Holy Spirit will move in you in wisdom, knowledge, and revelation. And when you stand to preach, it won't be your words; it will be what He taught you.*[1]

This word changed my life! I spent time in the quiet place with my journal and Bible to develop the ability to hear my Father. I had to pay a price for this intimacy then, and 30 years later, I continue to be in His

THE HEART OF A SON

presence each day. Ask yourself, "What kind of intimacy am I pursuing with Him?" Remarkably, when I get into His presence, I have heard the voice of my Father say that HE LOVES IT!

My place of intimacy with the Lord started in my bedroom by quieting my soul to hear His voice. I remember one time asking the Lord, "Is it You speaking to me, the devil, or is this all from the pizza I ate last night?"

The Lord spoke to me with an example. He said, "Think about when your wife or children call you on the phone; do you need to ask who it is?"

"No," I answered, "because I know their voice."

God replied, "Obviously, you are not spending enough time with Me, or you would recognize My voice when I speak to you!"

OUCH! His reply strongly impressed me, and I never forgot it. The result of spending time with God is the assurance of knowing His voice is speaking to you.

The key to being a son is to honor your Father by spending time with Him every day early in the morning. Over the years, I have been very active and sometimes slack off in this quiet time. But once I come back into His presence, I realize how much I missed being with my Father. Currently in my life, I am with Him early each morning, praying in tongues and then listening to that small, still voice speak to me. There is power in your Heavenly tongue language; it quiets your soul so your spirit can hear. I know that I must discipline myself and pay the price to hear my Father's voice.

> **HONOR YOUR FATHER BY SPENDING TIME WITH HIM EVERY DAY EARLY IN THE MORNING**

PRESENCE OF SONS

But you, beloved, build yourselves up [founded] on your most holy faith [make progress, rise like an edifice higher and higher], praying in the Holy Spirit.
JUDE 1:20 AMPC

People who have intimacy with God the Father have different motives, and there are different levels of your closeness to the Lord. Below are several descriptions and levels of intimacy with the Lord.

1. SUPERFICIAL INTIMACY: when we only come to God when we're in need of Him, especially during times of trials and crisis.

2. TRANSACTIONAL INTIMACY: when we treat God based on a transaction to acquire an exchange of something we desire. Example: Once you heal me, I'll follow You.

3. REFERRAL INTIMACY: when our relationship is based on what others say about God.

4. PERSONAL INTIMACY: when our relationship is based on the conviction that we have as we encounter Him personally.

5. SIGNAL INTIMACY: when our deep intimacy with God produces action from us. We begin to produce the fruit of our love toward God. A signal means something that incites to action.

6. PRINCIPAL INTIMACY: a personal relationship with God that has been built in a certain period and results in a principle, or pattern, that gets passed down to future generations. Example: Our focus is to teach our grandchildren how to hear God and fulfill their destiny on earth.[2]

THE HEART OF A SON

And the Lord spoke unto Moses face to face, as a man speaketh unto his friend. And he turned again into the camp: but his servant Joshua, the son of Nun, a young man, departed not out of the tabernacle.

EXODUS 33:11 KJV

When examining the life of Joshua, we can see that because of his desire to seek and stay in God's presence, the results proved the power of His presence in Joshua's life! Look at these testimonies from the book of Joshua:

GOD FIGHTS FOR YOU

And ye have seen all that the Lord your God hath done unto all these nations because of you; for the Lord your God is He that hath fought for you.

JOSHUA 23:3 KJV

GOD PROVIDES AN INHERITANCE

Behold, I have divided unto you by lot these nations that remain, to be an inheritance for your tribes, from Jordan, with all the nations that I have cut off, even unto the great sea westward. And the Lord your God, He shall expel them from before you, and drive them from out of your sight; and ye shall possess their land, as the Lord your God hath promised unto you.

JOSHUA 23:4-5 KJV

PRESENCE OF SONS

NOT ONE THING WILL FAIL

And behold, this day I am going the way of all the earth. Know in all your hearts and in all your souls that not one thing has failed of all the good things which the Lord your God promised concerning you. All have come to pass for you; not one thing of them has failed.
JOSHUA 23:14 AMPC

In our pursuit of God, there must be a cleaving to the Lord with a real, fervent love—what we identify as PASSION for Him. Passion is defined as an object of desire or deep interest, an intense, driving, or overmastering feeling, ardent affection: love, a strong liking or desire for or devotion to some activity, object, or concept. Our prototype in the New Covenant is Jesus. First, He would ascend the mountain, or choose a solitary place to hear His Father's voice in His Presence; then, He would come down to demonstrate the Kingdom of God.

What stops us from coming into oneness with God in His Presence? Time is the main issue! Distractions keep us from His presence. Emails, social media, apps on our iPads, continual texting, working longer hours coupled with more demands, our kids' sports schedule (particularly activities scheduled during Sunday services which I fully disagree with), and our daily routines. Somehow, some way, do we practically prioritize focusing on His presence with the endeavor to become one with Him? There is nothing like the Holy Spirit's whisper to me that reveals how much He loves it when I press into His presence.

My spiritual covering and spiritual father, Dr. Mark Kauffman, has written two great books entitled ***The Presence Driven Leader*** and ***Kings Arise***. If you want to improve your ability to hear the voice of God, be a presence-driven person, and find your identity as a king, then you need to purchase and study his books.[3]

THE HEART OF A SON

CONSIDER YOUR FOCUS

What if you took the next 40 days and began to focus on His presence? Forty days of Focus is a powerful principle to implement in your life. Create a focused environment and get away with the Lord. Personally, I get up around 5:30 AM, pray in tongues for 30 minutes, and just spend time in the presence of God the Father. Our spiritual father has a daily King's Table prayer meeting from 7:30 to 8:30 AM Monday – Friday that keeps us focused on the assignments that God has given us as a local church. Others I know who work in the marketplace give God a full day once a week, 8-5 PM, by getting away to a secluded area to pray, fast, read the Word, and listen to God's voice. They come out with strategies and answers to advance His Kingdom.

Are you too busy? That is what we hear from many people, but that is also why they are not seeing the manifestations of God's Kingdom in their lives because they lack intimacy in God's presence. Never excuse yourself from His presence!

O Lord, I love the habitation of Your house,
and the place where Your glory dwells.
PSALM 26:8 AMP

My whole being shall be satisfied as with marrow
and fatness; and my mouth shall praise You with
joyful lips When I remember You upon my bed
and meditate on You in the night watches.
PSALM 63:5, 6 AMPC

I have multiple testimonies of God's goodness manifesting in health, finances, and relationships. Because of my intimate relationship with God, the Lord has led me to my spiritual father, who has covered my family and me in every battle I have faced!

PRESENCE OF SONS

HEALTH

The Lord's voice guided me through an ordeal with my health. I had major pain while going to the bathroom and had blood in my urine. The Lord told me this was nothing to worry about, and after six months of doctors' visits and getting scoped, they discovered a small pouch of puss in my bladder area. The doctors tried to tell me I had a fistula, a permanent abnormal passageway between two organs in the body or between an organ and the exterior of the body.

They attempted to convince me I had a hole between my bladder and colon and wanted to perform major surgery to cut my colon back by 12 inches. I told the doctor to go in and take the pocket of puss out, which would resolve the issue. He did what I asked, and nothing has ever affected me again. Why? Initially in this process, I heard the voice of God declare to me that this issue was nothing and not to get surgery. I obeyed the voice of the Lord, remained covered by my spiritual father, and received my healing! Hearing His voice comes from time spent in His presence!

BIRTHDAY GIFT

Spending time in God's presence allows us to recognize when He is speaking to us and discern His voice from our own thoughts. When I was downsized from the Fortune 100 Company I worked for in the 1990s; I went to work for another individual for three years. In this time, my income level dropped significantly, and I had to rely on God for provision to build this new business and career program. On my birthday, I was driving near a local mall, and I heard God's voice tell me that the shirts I liked to wear and purchase for the usual price of $35 each were on sale for $6.99 each. God said He wanted to bless me. I turned my car around and went into the store. Sure enough, there were those dress shirts I

THE HEART OF A SON

liked at a retail price of $35 each. Above the shirts was a sale sign that said $9.99. I asked the clerk if the shirts were on sale, and she confirmed that they were on sale for $9.99. This may sound crazy, but I knew God had told me they were $6.99, so I asked her, "Are you sure that is the correct sales price?"

She said, "Oh yeah, I forgot to tell you that my manager came in this morning and told me to reduce all the shirts down to $6.99, but I have not had time to change the price."

I was able to buy five shirts for the price of one! See how good God is? But I had to be able to hear the voice of God, or I would have driven right past this opportunity and missed the blessing.

JOB AND RAISE

The Lord can speak to us more specifically by being a son of His presence. During a special church service, I heard the Lord tell me to ask my boss for three specific things. First, that I would get a new position in the company as Senior National Sales Representative. Second, that I would get a $10,000 raise since I was already selling and managing more volume than the other Senior National Sales Representatives. And finally, I should ask for a reduction in my territory responsibilities since I was managing an area that was too large for one person. I heard God say to believe for it within the next 30 days!

I had a choice to follow God's voice and boldly ask for these requests or to put it off and never follow through. I was confident that I heard the voice of the Lord; I was also physically drained and stressed out managing all these people in this large territory. I went to my spiritual father at the time, and one of the elders, and I submitted what I heard to get their counsel. They felt a quickening and a peace that this was from God and told me to go for it.

PRESENCE OF SONS

My first step was to turn to the Lord about how to do this. I prayed for boldness, and that week during my flight to the headquarters, I asked the Lord to prepare the way for me. I thought of my spiritual father covering me as I stepped out in faith and boldness. That night, my boss and I were the only two remaining in the office. I went to him and laid down a piece of paper with all the facts on it, what I was currently doing for the company, and my three requests. I told him I wanted to be more productive and drive more profit for the company, but since my territory was so big, I felt I did not have the time to accomplish these results. I asked him if it was possible for him to review my three requests within the next 30 days. I left that night with great confidence in God's message to me and expected Him to confirm this word.

About three weeks later, I received a call from my boss. He reviewed my requests, and the company valued me as a loyal employee. He would grant my requests in the 30-day period. I was promoted to senior manager; I received a $10,000 raise, and a reduction of territory—all because I acted on what I heard from the Lord! What a God we serve! Everything can change if you can begin to focus on His presence.

> I LEFT WITH GREAT CONFIDENCE AND EXPECTED GOD TO CONFIRM HIS WORD TO ME

I want to personally encourage you in the next 40 days to focus on spending time in God's presence and develop a lifestyle of intimacy with Him. Couple this with receiving from your spiritual father as well. In God's presence, meditate on what your spiritual father is teaching you. Reflect on his messages and devotions. This is time well spent in the Lord's presence, focusing on how God is moving in your local house of God and in your life.

THE HEART OF A SON

One thing have I asked of the Lord, that will I seek, inquire for, and [insistently] require: that I may dwell in the house of the Lord [in His presence] all the days of my life, to behold and gaze upon the beauty [the sweet attractiveness and the delightful loveliness] of the Lord and to meditate, consider, and inquire in His temple.

PSALM 27:4 AMPC

PRACTICAL FOCUS FOR PRESENCE

1. DEVELOP INTIMACY: I applied this principle of intimacy and the Word of God from Mrs. Pickett. I would get up in my bedroom, or a quiet place, with my Bible and journal to spend hours in His presence and write down everything He told me. The creation of Focus Life Institute[4] and the courses I have developed for Education, Business, Personal Growth, Professional Development, and Recovery/Reentry all came from spending time in His presence. By putting Him first place daily, your life will be an explosion of His almightiness! What can you begin to do this week to craft a more intimate relationship with the Lord?

2. ELIMINATE DISTRACTIONS: We need to shut down the outside world and get into a focused environment. Moses and Joshua were meeting God in a focused environment, and when they came out, they were able to accomplish the will of God. You will get what is needed to accomplish your destiny after you spend time in His presence! What can you limit or shut off that is distracting you from being with Him?

3. RECEIVE INSTRUCTION: What is your spiritual father been teaching you? Reflect on how the input from your spiritual father

causes you to accelerate and increase. What specific truths are you learning from him now?

4. IDENTIFY GIFTS: For my gifting, skill, and talents to rise to the next level, I must enter His presence so His grace and glory can overtake my natural abilities. List the natural gifts that God has given you and pray over them that He may increase them to their full potential.

5. TAKE TERRITORY: Once you develop your personal, intimate relationship in His Presence, your sensitivity will increase for others. Kingdom conquest is reclaiming, reforming, and subduing the world around us for the Kingdom of God. By spending time in His presence, your gifting and anointing will begin to produce the fruit that God wants for your territory. Do you have a heart for your city and those you minister to? What does God want you to do to advance His Kingdom where He has planted you?

6. SHOW UP: You are part of a Kingdom that will impact and change the world! In fact, creation is waiting for you! Study this Scripture and describe what it means in your life.

> *For the earnest expectation of the creature waiteth*
> *for the manifestation of the sons of God*
> ROMANS 8:19 KJV

7. COMMIT TO GROW: To be a true son, you need to have a presence-driven life and develop a personal quiet time and focused environment to fellowship with your Father. After successfully changing your habits to develop an intimate relationship with God, journal the changes you see in your life and the testimonies that result from them.

THE HEART OF A SON

ENDNOTES

1. For more information about the life of Mrs. Pickett, visit: https://ministrytodaymag.com/index.php/features/8628-a-teacher-and-a-mother
2. Source Unknown.
3. Dr. Mark Kauffman's books, *The Presence Driven Leader* and *Kings Arise* can be found at www.drmarkkauffman.org and on www.amazon.com.
4. The Focus Life Institute offers many great courses. You can find them all at www.focuslifeinstitute.com.

CHAPTER TWO
PURPOSE OF SONS

"Your purpose is your possession."
DR. MARK KAUFFMAN

Did you ever ask yourself, "Why do I exist?" Rest assured, God has a purpose for every life. There is no fulfillment without purpose. Many people have climbed the ladder of success only to discover that the ladder leans against the wrong wall. Once you recognize your purpose, you can begin to piece together what is necessary to fulfill that purpose. You can position yourself to hear, "Well done, my good and faithful servant" (Matthew 25:23).

Purpose embodies why you exist. Many of us have put purpose before presence. Everything starts with an intimate relationship with God in His presence, and then purpose is birthed from hearing His voice. *"For many are called, but few are chosen"* (Matthew 22:14 KJV). In other words, when you know you have a calling, then you need to choose to follow it.

In 1988, I realized there was more to discover in God, and I had to choose to either stay in religion or move into the realm of the Kingdom! You will need to make that choice along the journey of life. Choose well!

THE HEART OF A SON

From 1988 to 1999, we began to understand the Kingdom of God. Our son suffered a dirt bike accident on 9/11/99, which forced us to go to the next level in our faith. We needed a miracle, and we needed to find the place where God would position us for it to happen. With spiritual counsel, we relocated to a different church until 2008, whose focus was faith and healing. During these nine years, God opened the door for me to submit myself to apostolic leaders and to learn more about this new realm. We had to make a further choice – to move to the next level or stay in a place that was more of a pastoral domain, lacking the apostolic anointing. But in 2008, we were led to a new church by apostolic counsel and prophetic direction; we found "our bones" in this new church family and discovered our spiritual father/covering required to clarify and fulfill the purpose for our lives. Without the clarity from this apostolic covering, I would have remained frustrated, continuing to circle the same mountain.

Many friends and family did not follow us on this path, but here is where we found our destiny and purpose. There was and is a price to pay to enter the Kingdom of God.

> *Confirming the souls of the disciples, and exhorting them to continue in the faith, and that we must through much tribulation enter into the Kingdom of God.*
> ACTS 14:22 KJV

In September of 2004, my friend, Patrick Ondrey, told me to pray for strategic relationships to come my way. After 40 days of focused prayer, I connected with the International Coalition of Apostles under Apostle John Kelly, who became my spiritual father for that time and season. God began to raise me up within this organization to be a speaker in many roundtable discussions and wealth builders' conferences. I needed an

PURPOSE OF SONS

apostle to move to the next level, and I thank Apostle Kelly for speaking into my life and connecting me to other apostolic people.

In January 2005, I was asked to join a team of leaders in Minneapolis to discuss wealth transfer. This is where I met Bishop Bart Pierce from Rock City Church in Baltimore, Maryland. As my mentor, he provided me with the counsel and direction I needed to enter the Kingdom assignment and purpose for my life.

We each have a purposeful assignment. Most people do not see many results in their life because they are not focused on their assignment! When opportunities arise, be sure that it complements your assignment. An assignment is an undertaking or duty that you have been assigned to perform or do. An opportunity is a chance or a possibility of a favorable circumstance. A chance is described as a risk involving danger. Many people jump on any opportunity they encounter without seeking counsel to verify if it aligns with their life's assignment. It is critical to put your attention to what God has assigned you to accomplish.

Under these apostolic men, I was able to write my first book, entitled **The Focus Fulfilled Life**. With their apostolic anointing covering me and the Holy Spirit's insight from the quiet place, I also developed a variety of instructional and practical courses from my experiences related to God's Word.

> *Think over these things I am saying [understand them and grasp their application], for the Lord will grant you full insight and understanding in everything.*
> 2 TIMOTHY 2:7 AMPC

Once I had learned more about my message and assignment, God opened up doors to for me to speak in multiple churches in the United States to equip people to FOCUS.

THE HEART OF A SON

In 2008, I received spiritual counsel from both Apostle John Kelly and Bishop Bart Pierce to go to the next level to fulfill the purpose and assignment in my life. I knew I was called to train and change generations, but this demanded the right apostolic and spiritual covering to enter into my purpose. They knew the place for me to find my destiny was at Jubilee Ministries International Church in New Castle, PA. Drs. Mark and Jill Kauffman became our spiritual father and mother. Under them, we have gained greater revelation of our identity as a priest, prophet, king, and as a son of God.

Dr. Mark Kauffman's books, **The Presence Driven Leader** and **Kings Arise: The Kingmaker Anointing,** have changed my life. I never understood my identity until I came under his ministry and now, I know who I am, what I am called to do, and how to do it. He taught me how to operate in the priestly, prophetic, and kingly anointings as a son of God! When I read his book, **Kings Arise**, I could not stop weeping because it clearly identified my life's purpose. Your spiritual father will do exactly this; you will discover who you were always meant to be and what you were always meant to do.

Being under the Kauffman's ministry has led my wife, children, and grandchildren into our purposes and destinies! My granddaughter is a prime example of this. Our church has a flag and dance team that powerfully expresses praise and worship every Sunday at our celebration service. Since age 2, my granddaughter Elia has been watching their choreography and learning how to use flags. She enrolled in dance classes at age 6. Each week, she rehearsed the songs from that Sunday's service with flags and dancing. When she was 5-6 years old, she knew many of the moves to the songs, keeping up with the team during services. Her goal when she grew up was to be a "flagger." Drs. Mark and Jill Kauffman noticed her interest and often encouraged her in it. Of her own volition, she began attending the early Sunday morning rehearsals with the flag team to practice and learn. She knew her assignment one day would include being a flag/dance team member.

At age 7, Elia really combined her praise and worship with flagging/dance. Her worshipful expressions exploded! In services and at home, she sang with all her heart with her hands raised in genuine worship to the Lord. Her relationship with the Lord deepened during this time. Noticing these changes, Drs. Mark and Jill asked her parents' permission if she could be on the Jubilee Flag/Dance team. Of course, they said yes! She is so excited to express her praise and worship to the Lord with this new role. Spiritual covering is not just for adults. We can teach our children how to grow as a son of God and see Him move greatly in their lives. Elia's identity in Christ is being established, even at a young age. Establishing identity in Christ is a major result of those in a deep relationship with God and submitted to their spiritual covering.

> ESTABLISHING IDENTITY IN CHRIST IS A MAJOR RESULT OF THOSE IN A DEEP RELATIONSHIP WITH GOD AND SUBMITTED TO THEIR SPIRITUAL COVERING

You need an apostle to bring you into the fullness of your assignment and purpose. Submit to the spiritual father God has placed in your life and see your assignment come to life! I know this by experience and from testimonies of those under a set man/woman of God. Because I am a son under my spiritual father, I have been able to outline the purpose for my business, The Focus Life Institute. It is to educate, equip, and empower individuals to focus on identifying their personal callings and assignments in life, achieving their purpose, and fulfilling their destiny! In 2012, God began to deal with me from the word He gave me when I was downsized in 1995. For the next five years, the Holy Spirit revealed to me in the focused environment how to create courses to train and change generations create practical, online courses to help people in the areas of personal growth, professional development, K-12 educational curriculum, college retention and workplace preparation, recovery, and reentry for incarcerated individuals. The church is here to invade and impact the 7 cultural spheres of society (business, government, education, family, media, church, arts and entertainment) for the glory of God. You will know where you are called to in these spheres more clearly and definitively as a son.

CONSIDERING YOUR PURPOSE

The point of this exercise is to help you put your finger on the pulse of your own life and define what brings you joy and fulfillment. This unlocks opportunities for you to plan how to develop skills and acquire the education and experiences you need to make a living doing what you love.

- Review signposts along the way of your life that will help you understand your purpose. A signpost is a specific experience you encounter that gives you that feeling of success or gratification. For example, I am a people person. I love to be around people and do not have a fear of speaking in front of a crowd. That was a signpost that helped me in the business sphere as a manager in Fortune 100. In addition, it eventually led me into public speaking to help people focus.

- Review notable experiences in your life—your inner voice, people who have spoken into your life, books, or areas of interest.

- Review your strengths and areas that bring fulfillment.

- List some of your natural abilities as purpose will align with these.

PURPOSE OF SONS

The Bible says that many are called, but few choose to go all the way to make Him Lord of their lives. It is one thing to say He is your Savior, but you dive to a deeper level when He becomes Lord over your life! Align your purpose with the will of God but also to the corporate vision of your local church that you attend. Become involved and participate with the vision. How can your purpose, strengths, and talents help accomplish what God has called your local Body to do?

When you combine your purpose statement with your vision, then your mission of how you will achieve this comes into view. Everyone's purpose statement will be different. There are no wrong answers. Unlock opportunities to plan how to develop your skills and acquire the education and experience you need to make a living by doing what you love while advancing God's Kingdom!

MY PERSONAL PURPOSE EXAMPLES

- My purpose is to be a Focus Coach to train up this generation to identify their personal assignments, fulfill their God-given destinies and positively influence society!
- My purpose is to be an entrepreneur to create an agency fueled by confidence and passion to help your company grow.

Why did God put you on the planet for this time? The answer is your purpose. There is a difference between a vision, purpose, and mission statement.

- VISION explains where you are going in life.
- PURPOSE reveals why you exist.
- MISSION describes how you will get there.

THE HEART OF A SON

You must come under a spiritual father for covering and embrace the process of purpose. The definition of process is a series of actions or steps taken to achieve a particular end. You must enjoy the process along the journey.

> *Consider it wholly joyful, my brethren, whenever you are enveloped in or encounter trials of any sort or fall into various temptations. Be assured and understand that the trial and proving of your faith bring out endurance and steadfastness and patience. But let endurance and steadfastness and patience have full play and do a thorough work, so that you may be [people] and fully developed [with no defects], lacking in nothing.*
> JAMES 1:2-4 AMPC

You must spend time in God's presence since our main purpose is to be intimate with Him and our destiny is to manifest Him in the earth. In this quiet place of a focused environment with God, He will instruct you to fulfill your purpose.

PRACTICAL FOCUS FOR PURPOSE

1. Spend time with the Lord over the next several days to define the following:

   - VISION (where you are going):

   - PURPOSE (why you exist):

   - MISSION (how you will get there):

PURPOSE OF SONS

2. Our purpose can be revealed over time, and pieces of it come together like a puzzle:
    - Write a testimony or bullet the main events of your life to show the steps God has brought you through to this moment where you are defining your life to advance His Kingdom and to give Him glory.

THE HEART OF A SON

WE MUST SPEND TIME IN GOD'S PRESENCE SINCE OUR MAIN PURPOSE IS TO BE INTIMATE WITH HIM AND OUR DESTINY IS TO MANIFEST HIM IN THE EARTH.

CHAPTER THREE
PREPARATION OF SONS

Preparation is never wasted! God always leads sons through a preparation process to grow and increase in the Kingdom of God. You will need to be prepared as a son to enter in and help facilitate the vision of your set man and woman of God. However, you must also prepare yourself for what you must endure to see the release of God's provision over your assignment in life. When Moses led the children of Israel out of Egypt in Exodus 12, the Lord instructed Moses to prepare the people. These specific directions led them into their destiny to exit Egypt after the first Passover. Similarly, we must follow the Lord's instructions to be prepared for the divine destinies that He has given us.

> PREPARATION—the act or operation of preparing or fitting for a particular purpose, use, service or condition; *(Webster's 1828 Dictionary).*

THE HEART OF A SON

Consider these two Scriptures regarding preparation:

> *The preparations of the heart in man, and the answer of the tongue, is from the Lord.*
> PROVERBS 16:1 KJV

> *Establishing and strengthening the souls and the hearts of the disciples, urging and warning and encouraging them to stand firm in the faith, and [telling them] that it is through many hardships and tribulations we must enter the Kingdom of God.*
> ACTS 14:22 AMPC

After graduating college in 1977, I interviewed for my first job in an economy that was still recovering from the severe 1973-75 recession. I sent out more than 150 letters to companies and received 150 rejection letters. However, just prior to graduation, I was invited to spend two weeks in Jackson and Mendenhall, Mississippi, to volunteer and serve at the Voice of Calvary Ministries under Dr. John Perkins. Dr. Perkins is a Christian minister, civil rights activist, Bible teacher, best-selling author, philosopher, and community developer.

Here we were, five white guys and our leader volunteering in the black community; it was an experience that changed our lives forever. God used this to prepare me for what I would encounter in future relationships by helping me understand the love of God for my brothers in Christ. This experience also taught me how to get along with people who had a different culture from mine. I had many African American friends in high school and college, but on that trip, I was across the railroad tracks living in their environment. By listening to and spending time in the home of Dr. Perkins, his wife Vera Mae, and their children, we experienced something very special. It was unique to see this man's vision change the lives and environment in his sphere of influence in that territory.

He taught us about the pain he endured from the fatal shooting of his brother, Clyde, and how he left Mississippi. Responding to the call of God, he returned to his hometown to make a difference. He shared about the cycle of money and how to keep it circulating in the black community to build that economy. He explained that in 1970, he was arrested and tortured for his stand for racial equality. And by the mid-seventies, Voice of Calvary, Jackson and Mendenhall Ministries were operating thrift stores, health clinics, a housing cooperative, and classes in Bible and theology. Perkins was in demand as a speaker in evangelical churches, colleges, and conventions across the country. His testimony has remained with me all these years.

When I returned home, I was changed. I grew in my ability to love and work with all types of people, environments, and cultures. I went to work for General Tire and Rubber Company and trained to be a manager in a retail store in Erie, PA. However, I never had peace about taking this job and believed God had something different in mind. After six weeks, I went to my boss and explained my feelings about working there, and since he was a Christian, he understood my spiritual dilemma and released me from the company.

GOD HAD A DIFFERENT PLAN

My mother sent my resume to Lever Brothers (Division of Unilever, the largest package goods company in the world at that time). While working at a retail shoe store, I got a call for an interview for a local sales position. I was told I was one of 120 people who submitted a resume for that position.

THE HEART OF A SON

At that time, I was studying Hebrews 11, the faith chapter. I had two interviews with the company and shared my experiences in Mississippi. I found myself in the running for the position. While reading Hebrews 11 on a Friday morning, I just released my faith for that position. I got up and took a shower, and I heard in my spirit, "I am giving you that job; you got it!" I called my fiancé (who, shortly after that, became my wife) and told her God's word about the job! Cindy asked, "What are you going to do about it?"

I decided to call Bob, my would-be boss, to tell *him* I got the job. Confidently, I had heard the inner witness, and boldness rose in me to make that call; this was my revelation. Bob related that I was one of three that the team was still reviewing. He asked me how I knew I got the job, and I said, "I just knew it."

Well, on Monday morning, I got the call and was prepared to start my career in Fortune 100 that would last for over 37 years with Unilever for ten years and the Coca-Cola Company as a manager and trainer for over 27 years.

God prepared me for my assignment through every step along the way. My final destination was not in Erie, PA managing a tire store. God had a different plan. It was the beginning of working for worldwide and nationally known companies with leaders that see things in a higher and different realm.

Coca-Cola has evangelized the world with a soft drink. Over the years, attending the meetings of these top companies caused me to think and act differently. I was being prepared at a high level of training to work with millions of dollars in my sphere of influence and bring the Kingdom principles into these arenas. The results were producing great levels of success. While these companies display apostolic and prophetic cultural elements, they fail to embrace the Kingdom cause as their focus.

PREPARATION OF SONS

During this time, I was involved in a local, denominational church in leadership as an elder and other functions. Although I was heavily involved in church activities, I was simply "playing church." There was also a distinct lack of teaching of present-day truth. God began to deal with me to change. Since I was on the road 2-3 days per week, it was evident that I was not living for the Lord. In 1987, I got a call that Lever Brothers had bought another company, and they were going with a broker sales force, thus eliminating my direct sales force team that reported to me as their manager. To keep my job, I was asked to relocate, but I felt God would provide something better for me, just like He had in the past. I was to work until the middle of August and then be downsized with a severance package.

I saw a Coca-Cola Foods division job available, and I flew to Houston, Texas, to interview for the position with twelve leaders in the organization. God had already prepared me as I identified specific areas where I believed I could help improve their current situation in the local marketplace. I audited over 100 stores and brought in my findings. I was hired in late July to start September 15, giving me a whole year's salary as a severance and a month off to be with my wife and children. God was preparing me for my next great adventure to advance His Kingdom in the earth!

After a few months, however, I was still not living for the Lord. But in February 1988, while I was in a hotel room, the Lord told me that if I did not CHANGE and move into what He had for me, I would lose everything. Ready to move on with more of God, I made a decision to follow Him. A few months later, we were invited to a local non-denominational church that believed in apostolic and prophetic ministries.

THE HEART OF A SON

ONE WORD FROM THE LORD

On the night of August 27, 1988, our lives changed. A prophet from Christian International in Florida under Dr. Bill Hamon was ministering that weekend. During the morning service, a man behind me said I needed to come back that night because the Prophet Gary Brooks would give me a prophetic word for my life. That night when the service had gone on for two hours, I looked at Cindy and said it was time to go. Sitting in the back row, I thought it would be easy to slip out to go pick up our two young children from her parents' house. She said adamantly that it was not time to go yet! A minute later, Prophet Brooks calls us out. "You two in the back come up here; God has a word for you," he said. That one word from God changed our lives forever and prepared us for our future. Here are the highlights from that word from the Lord that night:

- We thank you for the Word of the Lord, the mind of Christ being revealed to them to confirm, direct, and instruct. Speak to their hearts, oh God, confirm things, oh Lord. You know the questions, you know the wanderings, and Lord, you know the things on their hearts even this night. Lord God, we just thank You for the Word of the Lord; we release the prophetic anointing to flow.

- Father, we lay anointed hands on your anointed vessels. For son and daughter, I'm doing a new planting, I'm doing an uprooting now, and I'm releasing you. I'm going to bring you into a place that is going to be large in vision. The Lord God says, "You have been like two baby chicks sitting under a dead mother hen, and a ministry has not been able to come forth."

- But the Lord God says, "I'm going to send you to a place; you are going to be accepted, you're going to be loved, you're going to be restored, and there is going to be a proving time. You will observe like ministry, and I will put you to the test. But son and

PREPARATION OF SONS

daughter, I'm going to send you forth, and I'm getting ready to cause a stirring and that release to come forward. Go with my peace, go with my joy, leave in a proper manner, and do what I've told you to do. Go where I told you to go."

- For the Lord says, "Submit to authority, remain teachable. Take heed of the multitude of counsel that I would wrap and surround you with. For man of God, for as you work for others, for the day will come when you will see yourself moving in your own business." The Lord says, "I'm going to increase the finances, and there is going to be a blessing that I have for you."

- "Daughter, I am calling you to come out of your shell of timidity, for you're like a crab coming out of that shell. The Lord says I'm drawing you out, and I'm plugging you and putting you into a new river. I'm transplanting you, and you're going to flow in women's ministry. For a time and a season, I am going to have you both sitting like a sponge, receiving and absorbing the things of God. If you receive, I'll pour My spirit out to you and make My words known unto you. Daughter, you are a jewel in My Kingdom. Others have come and spoken words against you; they tried to tear you down and tried to speak vanities, but I would say you didn't give ear to it.

- "Things weighted you down, things went into your heart, but you have been dealing with these things. Know this, that the word of the Lord will cut assunder and remove all doubt and all fear and even this night." This sister has a healing anointing in her as she will heal the broken-hearted in the name of the Lord.

- I just see you all going down one pathway. And I just see God whispering into your ear and your spirit and saying it is time for the release. God is going to put you into a place of ministry, where there is going to be the present-day truth flowing. Apparently, you don't go here because this church is moving in present-day truth. But I just see a transplanting, and you just need to leave proper ethics wherever you may go or wherever you're going. Leave in a proper attitude, and in a right spirit. Let God move you into a new place and new territory that He is getting to send you forth.

- Brother, God has some leadership material in you. It is going to be a season of just a few years, He wants to make the man, and He is going to work in you, work through you, and God is going to raise you up in a local church. I see your wife just being a part of the dance company that God is going to raise up. I see her just being very athletic. I just see her that has a spirit of warfare within her, and you are just going to flow, you are going to catch on real quick, you are going to adapt, learn and adjust, things aren't going to be difficult as you think as they get blown up in your mind concerning praise and worship ministry. But you're going to adjust and fit right in, just like a piece of the puzzle, and fit right in. But God is getting to remove the veil, and He is going to let you look into the Holy of Holies. The things you desired, the things you have seen afar off, and it has not been clear in your understanding. The ministry of the Word, the ministry of the spirit, God is going to open up new avenues of understanding. To let you see and understand the present-day truth, the current move of God, and what He is doing in the church. Praise God.

This one word forever changed the life of our marriage, children, relatives, and eventually our grandchildren, who all are now on fire for God. We had to come under a new spiritual father to grow in the truths of the Kingdom of God. But according to the prophecy, we had to do the following so that God would pour out His Spirit on us to fulfill those promises.

- **God had to reveal to us our potential**—once we saw this potential, then we needed to release ourselves from the current church we were attending and move on with God. We began to go to this church that was preaching present-day truth.

- **Leave in a proper manner**—we went to our pastor and explained our situation, and he blessed us as "sent" ones, not "went" ones. Many people leave a church without being sent, and they become went ones who either got offended or had an issue with the pastor or another family. When you leave like that, God cannot and will not bless you. You will be taking that same offense into the next church without getting healed or bringing closure. We left with a proper attitude of love, and then I went back six months later and met my former pastor to follow up and remain on good terms.

- **Submit to authority**—we had to remain teachable and receive counsel from others in this new church. We submitted and plugged into a weekly house group ministry that helped us get started in our new adventure.

- **Be like a sponge**—the prophet told us to sit like a sponge, receive, and absorb the things of God. For two years, we sat and were taught the principles of the Kingdom and God began to pour out His spirit on us, including our children.

- **Relinquish doubt**—when we left the former church, I was receiving phone calls from other members saying, "Who do you think you are? Are you too good for us?" We were literally shunned and talked about negatively within the church where we served for over ten years. They tried to tear my wife and I down, but we knew we heard God and would not give any attention to it.

- **Result**—by following through, God had promised to bring us into leadership. This happened in several areas.

God prepared us in those two years for the next twelve years as we served at this local church under our spiritual father at that time. The results of that preparation time where we absorbed the things of God are as follows:

- In two years, I was raised up to sing on the worship team, and within six years I was one of the worship leaders ushering people into the presence of God.
- In three years, we were raised up as House Group leaders and eventually had the largest house group of over 50 people and 20 kids. Witnessing multiple miracles and signs during this time, we saw God ignite several families with excitement for His Kingdom as they served within the church.
- My wife became the treasurer of the church and was raised up as a top intercessor, served on the dance and worship signing team as well as led the House Group with me.
- After six years, we were positioned as the House Group Team overseeing six House Groups in the church.
- We were part of building the church's Christian school and added grades 7-12 for a full K-12 private school option in the area to educate young people for their future.
- I was raised up as a leader of the Christian Business Counsel, a group of over 80 people with an anointing in business. We had monthly meetings and mentored multiple business leaders to find success in their callings.

PREPARATION OF SONS

- My children were part of a ministry started by Pastor Helen Beason called S.W.A.T. (Spiritual Warfare Advanced Training). They traveled on teams to minister to children and adults in churches throughout the Midwest, northeastern states, and southeastern states. My daughter, Theresa, led worship playing the keyboard, and my son, Daniel, was preaching and in flag ministry.

Obeying the voice of the Lord and making this one change—leaving family and loved ones behind in order to move on with God—prepared us for what was coming in our life. Remember, the time you put into preparation is never wasted!

PRACTICAL FOCUS FOR PREPARATION

1. When God says to move, you need to move. If you are called to go to another church, leave properly, and get a blessing when you leave. You need to find your "bones" (a.k.a. your spiritual DNA) that you're meant to be connected to.

> *But now hath God set the members every one*
> *of them in the body, as it hath pleased Him.*
> 1 CORINTHIANS 12:18 KJV

- Are you currently in this position of being ready to move into more of God in a new place, or has this already happened to you? Share your experiences.

THE HEART OF A SON

2. You must be prepared to sacrifice everything to get in the will of God.

    - Make a list of what you believe you can surrender to the Lord. What needs to go to make more room for Him?

3. Learn how to submit to authority, be teachable, and receive correction and counsel from those in leadership.

    - Do you struggle with being teachable and submitting to another's authority? Pray and ask the Lord why that is. Journal what He reveals to you with new thinking patterns and how He intends for you to receive well from others.

4. You MUST get involved in the local church, be ready to train and learn, and look for areas to SERVE.

    - Identify your giftings and anointing and serve the local church and community.
    - Make a chart of your gifts and talents.
    - What area would you be excited to serve in at your local church?
    - How has God prepared you for this moment?

CHAPTER FOUR
PERFECTION OF SONS

While praying in my focused environment, I asked the Lord what I could do to love and serve Him better. His response was just, "BE MY SON!" A son of God must operate in agape love (the highest expression of love). First, prioritize your love for God, His presence, and love for others. Agape love is unconditional love. Just like we love our natural children, we need to have the love for our Heavenly, earthly, and spiritual fathers.

> *Then one of them, which was a lawyer, asked Him a question, tempting Him, and saying, "Master, which is the great commandment in the law?" Jesus said unto him, "Thou shalt love the Lord thy God with all thy heart, and with all thy soul, and with all thy mind. This is the first and great commandment. And the second is like unto it, Thou shalt love thy neighbour as thyself. On these two commandments hang all the law and the prophets."*
> MATTHEW 22:35-40 KJV

THE HEART OF A SON

My dog, Blaze, is a golden retriever, and every morning while I am in the presence of God in my focused environment, here comes Blaze begging for love! So, I take a few minutes to scratch under his chin and ears. Each day he smiles as he gets his daily love fix. In fact, this happens about 2-3 times a day. One morning, the Lord said, "Do you ever deny that dog any love?"

I replied, "Never."

God said, "When you come into My presence, do you think I will ever deny you? No, I will never deny a son who comes into My presence seeking My face and needing My love. Love is the key to being a son! BE MY SON!"

Let us then approach God's throne of grace with confidence, so that we may receive mercy and find grace to help us in our time of need.
HEBREWS 4:16 NIV

THE HEART OF THE FATHER IS TO CHANGE YOU AND PERFECT YOU INTO HIS LIKENESS TO REVEAL HIS NATURE

The heart of the Father is to CHANGE you and perfect you into His likeness to reveal His nature. Every one of your fathers—God the Father, your natural biological father, and your spiritual fathers want to see you come into perfection, or maturity, in all areas of your life. You are not required to do everything perfectly, but focus on growing and maturing in your faith journey with God's guidance.

PERFECTION OF SONS

But the God of all grace, who hath called us unto His eternal glory by Christ Jesus, after that ye have suffered a while, make you perfect, establish, strengthen, settle you.
1 PETER 5:10 KJV

And He gave some, apostles; and some, prophets; and some, evangelists; and some, pastors and teachers; For the perfecting of the saints, for the work of the ministry, for the edifying of the body of Christ: Till we all come in the unity of the faith, and of the knowledge of the Son of God, unto a perfect man, unto the measure of the stature of the fulness of Christ.
EPHESIANS 4:11-13 KJV

Now may the God who brought us peace by raising from the dead our Lord Jesus Christ so that He would be the Great Shepherd of His flock; and by the power of the blood of the eternal covenant may He work perfection into every part of you giving you all that you need to fulfill your destiny. And may He express through you all that is excellent and pleasing to Him through your life-union with Jesus the Anointed One who is to receive all glory forever! Amen!
HEBREWS 13:20-21 TPT

A son's heart must be towards the fathers God has placed in his life. Your heavenly Father, your spiritual father, and your natural father fall into this order, and all are vital for your life.

THE HEART OF A SON

HEAVENLY FATHER

Transforming and conforming to your Heavenly Father's image is the greatest way to honor Him and fulfill your life's highest calling and purpose. Our Father wants you and me to become one with Him.

> *That they all may be one; as thou, Father, art in Me, and I in Thee, that they also may be one in us: that the world may believe that Thou hast sent Me. And the glory which Thou gavest Me I have given them; that they may be one, even as We are one: I in them, and Thou in Me, that they may be made perfect in one; and that the world may know that Thou hast sent Me, and hast loved them, as Thou hast loved Me.*
> JOHN 17:21-23 KJV

> *For as many as are led by the Spirit of God, they are the sons of God.*
> ROMANS 8:14 KJV

When I am being led by the Holy Spirit, He helps me be transformed (Romans 12:2-3) and conformed to His image.

> *And we know that all things work together for good to them that love God, to them who are the called according to His purpose. For whom He did foreknow, He also did predestinate to be conformed to the image of His Son, that He might be the firstborn among many brethren.*
> ROMANS 8:28-29 KJV

There is so much found in these words. I have been meditating on these Scriptures for years because so much of our lives center on being conformed to His image, a process that takes time.

PERFECTION OF SONS

But you did not so learn Christ! Assuming that you have really heard Him and been taught by Him, as [all] Truth is in Jesus [embodied and personified in Him], Strip yourselves of your former nature [put off and discard your old unrenewed self] which characterized your previous manner of life and becomes corrupt through lusts and desires that spring from delusion; And be constantly renewed in the spirit of your mind [having a fresh mental and spiritual attitude], And put on the new nature (the regenerate self) created in God's image, [Godlike] in true righteousness and holiness.
EPHESIANS 4:20-24 AMPC

How do we please our Heavenly Father? By stripping off our old man and putting on the new nature of Christ. I am created in God's image, and through Christ, I can live a life of true righteousness and holiness! To be transformed into His image and Christ-likeness is only the beginning. We need to continue the ongoing process of working out our salvation.

Therefore, my dear ones, as you have always obeyed [my suggestions], so now, not only [with the enthusiasm you would show] in my presence but much more because I am absent, work out (cultivate, carry out to the goal, and fully complete) your own salvation with reverence and awe and trembling (self-distrust, with serious caution, tenderness of conscience, watchfulness against temptation, timidly shrinking from whatever might offend God and discredit the name of Christ). [Not in your own strength] for it is God Who is all the while effectually at work in you [energizing and creating in you the power and desire], both to will and to work for His good pleasure and satisfaction and delight.
PHILIPPIANS 2:12-13 AMPC

THE HEART OF A SON

In his book, ***Your Highest Calling,*** Bishop Bill Hamon of Christian International, offers the following suggestions to be transformed and conformed to His image by becoming Christlike in the following practical areas:

- Become Christlike in CHARACTER
- Become Christlike in RIGHTEOUSNESS
- Become Christlike in ATTITUDE
- Become Christlike in WORK
- Become Christlike in WISDOM
- Become Christlike in FAITH
- Become Christlike in HOLINESS
- Become Christlike in HUMAN RELATIONSHIPS
- Become Christlike in GROWTH AND MATURITY

It is a daily process and will take sacrifices to understand that our Heavenly Father is raising up a spotless Bride so He can establish His Kingdom upon the earth through us. Jesus is our perfect example of how He grew into his sonship (Luke 2:52). As the ultimate Son to His Father, He only did what He heard the Father tell Him to do. (John 5:18-19).

NATURAL FATHERS

Unfortunately, we are living in a time where there are many children living without their natural/birth fathers. A recent statistic says that children living in single-mother homes is the second most common U.S. living arrangement, a number that has doubled since 1968. About 7.6 million (11%) children lived with their mothers only in 1968 compared to 15.3 million (21%) in 2020. The lack of fathers has contributed to an orphan spirit commonly found among today's young people.

PERFECTION OF SONS

You may be asking yourself, "What is an orphan spirit?" It's a demonic spirit that invades a person's mind causing them a sense of abandonment from their past hurts and experiences. It attacks the mind and emotions of the individual suffering with abandonment, rejection, and great disappointment. An orphan spirit attaches to a person who has experienced extreme rejection in their life. It creates separation, worry, anxiety, and fear. Once this spirit enters into a person, it becomes a stronghold in their mind and remains there until a new foundational truth of the Word of God is formed (Source: Behind the Chair Ministries).

Due to an orphan spirit, it is difficult for people to submit to a spiritual father in their lives. Concerning this, my spiritual father says, "If you cannot submit to a spiritual father who you can see, how can you submit to God the Father whom you cannot see?"

My dad was 45 years old when I was born, and he worked as a Westinghouse inspector during the afternoon shift from 3-11 PM until he retired. That meant that my brother and I only saw our father on weekends since he was sleeping when we left for school and had gone to work when we got home. He missed all my little league baseball, junior and senior high football, and baseball games. Due to his work schedule, it was not until my college years that he could attend my football games.

Now, my dad loved us. As a young man, he fought in WWII in the Battle of the Bulge, returned home, and had to work in the steel mill to support his brothers through college since he was the oldest child. The responsibility to care for the family rested on him, which came down from his father. However, the one thing my dad instilled in me was that he was a man of the Word of God. He listened to multiple radio stations when he was home alone while my mother worked and began to move into the things of the Spirit until my mother told him to back off of those deeper truths. They were both Christians, loved God, and went

THE HEART OF A SON

around to churches singing; Mom played the piano and my dad his violin. However, my mother did not want to go deep into the things of God; she just wanted to maintain what she knew through her denomination. Later, when my family joined a non-denominational church, she thought we were in a cult! But, later in her life, when it was time to pray for her healing and minister to her in the hospital, guess who she called? My wife and me! God healed and delivered her multiple times.

When my father passed away in 1993, he was in a Veterans' hospital. I would go often and minister to him since he had dementia. I would bring the Word of God in his room, and he would perk right up and listen to me. My father's desire for more of God was the legacy I wanted from him, and that has continued on in my life.

In my own experience as a father, while working for Fortune 100 companies, the demand and stress were great, along with travel. I found myself coming home after being on the road for days, only to run down to my office to the awaiting paperwork. All the while, I never stopped to grab my wife and kids to tell them I missed them. The Lord spoke to me that the work for the company would never be completely accomplished. He further explained, "You could have something to do 24/7, but I want you to change your priorities and spend time with your wife and children. Do not be like your father but become the father your children need you to be."

From then on, I was outside playing whiffle ball and badminton, swimming with them, and coaching their sporting events. I had to make a choice to spend quality time with my children as their natural father. It was then much easier for them to relate to their Heavenly Father, and furthermore, they learned to submit to a spiritual father because of my example of love and commitment to them. I had to spend time with them in their presence and that made all the difference in developing a close relationship with them.

PERFECTION OF SONS

I submit to you, fathers—spend time with your kids and have fun with them and develop that personal relationship. This is time that you can never get back, so determine to use it well. Your work-life balance is critical in this day to include spending time with your family.

SPIRITUAL FATHERS

The function and the role of a spiritual father is first to bring forth the Word of God to CHANGE you into the nature of His image! Secondly, they have the responsibility to train, equip, and empower their spiritual sons to help fulfill the corporate vision of the local church and personal destinies. A father will nurture and protect a son. The spiritual father will pour out knowledge, understanding, wisdom, counsel, and blessing to the son. This father's primary goal is to make the son successful in knowing the Lord and fulfilling the call of God on the son's life. Spiritual fathers enjoy spending time with their sons, not out of obligation, but because they are truly family.

However, we live in a world that exalts people who operate in an independent spirit. Working in Fortune 100 for over 37 years as a manager and trainer, I have seen this spirit within many people, and I have had to combat it and expose it to get the people working for me. Doing so has launched me into a place of God's favor and blessing in my business. That meant I had to eliminate and fire some people who refused to change.

In the realm of the church, we see the same independent spirit operating. This mindset says: nobody is going to tell me what to do, only God! Are you serious? God always uses a set man and woman of God to disciple and build you up, tear down your weaknesses, and cover you in your day of battle! A true son will submit to a true spiritual father. Become a person who is teachable so you can grow and mature in the

THE HEART OF A SON

principles and patterns of the Kingdom. This is found repeatedly in the Word of God.

> *But now hath God set the members every one of them in the body, as it hath pleased him.*
> 1 CORINTHIANS 12:18 KJV

It is not where you are assigned to but to WHOM you are assigned. It is God who sets the members in His body. When you look at the biblical pattern, you see Abraham had his 381, David had his 400 men, Gideon had his 300, and Jesus had His 12. I am assigned to a spiritual father where God has positioned me to help fulfill the corporate vision. When I focus on fulfilling that vision, my personal assignment and destiny align to it so that both can be achieved.

I learned submission early in my life and to trust in God's ways instead of my own. In my family's history, I had to deal with Jezebel and manipulating spirits, but I decided to overcome these and submit to authority. When I was trained in prophetic workshops in our church from curriculum under Dr. Bill Hamon and Christian International, I practiced submission. When God would give me a prophetic word, I would submit it upwards in the proper protocol, and if they used the word or not, it did not matter. I was free from my part of it since I submitted it to leadership. I did not get offended or upset if things didn't go the way I wanted, but I followed the principles and patterns of the Kingdom.

This attitude of submission was so evident in my business while I managed 6 markets in the Great Lakes region at one point in my career. We have authority when we are under proper spiritual authority, much like how the military works. Because I had submitted to my spiritual authority, my employees also submitted to my authority. I built relationships with them based on friendship and support. There

PERFECTION OF SONS

were times to be sensitive when I needed to stop a meeting to pray for someone. There were multiple occasions where I was able to pray for those going through difficulties: a divorce, one whose son was shot five times from a drive-by shooting, and those who had faced cancers and other diseases. My business was my ministry! Since I was covered by my spiritual father, I could cover them since they were under me. Psalm 133 explains how this works under the commanded blessing. It all flows down from headship.

> *Behold, how good and how pleasant it is for brethren to dwell together in unity! It is like the precious ointment upon the head, that ran down upon the beard, even Aaron's beard: that went down to the skirts of his garments; As the dew of Hermon, and as the dew that descended upon the mountains of Zion: for there the Lord commanded the blessing, even life for evermore.*
> PSALM 133 KJV

The following Scripture is so true and powerfully related to submission. If you want to really understand the principles and patterns of the Kingdom, then operate in this truth.

> *And if ye have not been faithful in that which is another man's, who shall give you that which is your own?*
> LUKE 16:12 KJV

For over 45 years, my wife and I have been faithful to another man's vision, and God has given me my own! This spans from my time in a denominational church, a Pentecostal church, and at Jubilee Ministries International City Church. Since 2008, I found a Kingdom church with a true spiritual mother and father who have equipped and trained me

THE HEART OF A SON

to be transformed and conformed to the nature of the image of Christ! Like Jesus, I am a priest, prophet, king, and a son of God! In addition, I submitted myself to those spiritual mentors who have impacted our lives; however, our main focus is serving and submitting our time, talent, and treasure to my spiritual father and mother, Apostles Mark Jill Kauffman at Jubilee Ministries.

> *After all, though you should have ten thousand teachers (guides to direct you) in Christ, yet you do not have many fathers. For I became your father in Christ Jesus through the glad tidings (the Gospel).*
> 1 CORINTHIANS 4:15 AMPC

So how do you submit to a spiritual father? Here are a few protocols that you need to do to receive the commanded blessing of Psalms 133. Know the heart of your father and mother. When you enter into a covenant relationship with spiritual parents, it is all about the heart. I know how much my Apostles love my family and me and how we love them. In fact, we often say, "I love you with my life!" Are you at that point yet in your relationship with your spiritual father?

I wrote three books about Kingdom values and character development. These are what I call the lost virtues of our society. The first one is a faith-based book entitled **The HEROES Principle.** The second one for high schools, organizations, and the marketplace is **The HEROES Effect**. The final book, **Be A Hero, Empowering Youth to Influence Their World**, is a discipleship book for churches, youth groups, organizations, and clubs for schools. Following is a quick recap about these six powerful HEROES principles that will impact your life.

PERFECTION OF SONS

HEROES PRINCIPLES

1. **H**ONOR—gaining an understanding of the benefits of walking in honor and respecting others.
2. **E**XCELLENCE—identifying ways to step up your game and be the best you can be in any situation.
3. **R**ESPONSIBILITY—learning how to take a greater level of responsibility for your life's endeavors.
4. **O**RDER—gaining an understanding that order is needed in any situation to bring about the best results.
5. **E**XPECTATION—learning how to expect and attain greater results by increasing your level of expectation and fostering a positive outlook.
6. **S**ERVANTHOOD—identifying the personal benefits of serving others while gaining personal satisfaction through helping others.

These principles are difficult to find in today's society. We see dishonor everywhere. Most people do only what they are told to do and never go beyond to reach a spirit of excellence. There is a lack of personal responsibility called entitlement that is rampant in our society. Many are not submitted to any authority, and have a pessimistic attitude, and nobody wants to be a servant leader. They look after their own self-interests.

These six values are Kingdom principles and, if applied, can change your life by bringing great favor, increase, and influence to you. Let's review a few of these with Psalm 133 in mind. This is the culture that my spiritual father has incorporated within our church, and the result is God's presence and glory evident in every service. To achieve the results

THE HEART OF A SON

of Psalm 133, the commanded blessing, put these principles into practice with your spiritual father and mother.

HONOR

I honor the function of my spiritual parents by refusing to become familiar with them. They are not my buddies, my pals, nor do I call them by their first name. Now, I hear some religious people saying I am getting into legalism. No, this is about HONOR! Examine yourself—and look for honor in your life. You see, honor is equated with the highest degree of respect, mingled with awe, purposed for the dignity and character of another person. Those who show honor radiate a good reputation, good quality or character as judged by other people, and uphold high moral standards of behavior.

> **THOSE WHO SHOW HONOR RADIATE A GOOD REPUTATION**

If you cannot honor your set man and woman of God and see them as the ones God has placed within your life to CHANGE you to conform to the image of Christ, then you need to repent and ask God to show you ways to honor your spiritual father. This is why we see the church in its current condition with no power and filled with weak members not honoring those whom God has positioned them with to advance the Kingdom of God.

Honor is remiss in most circles today and, sad to say, especially in the church. Honor your spiritual parents as well as others by giving them respect. Value them as who they are and their responsibility from God to lead you into fulfilling your assignment, purpose, and destiny. That is why we call those in leadership by their function – Apostle, Prophet, Elder, Deacon, etc. It is the same when I was in the business realm by introducing my managers as Vice President or Director of Marketing, providing the honor and respect due to their function. The Scripture says that you reap what you sow! Because I walked in honor, I had influence at the Coca-Cola Company and held share leadership in my territory. This came about all because I honored my managers, peers, and customers.

We have an HONOR service at my church every year honoring someone who has made a spiritual impact in our community or in the advancement of the Kingdom. They sit in a special seat up front, flowers and gifts are showered upon them, and many words are spoken in their honor. It is a wonderful method to honor men and women who have greatly affected our communities by executing their Kingdom assignments. As my spiritual father, Dr. Mark Kauffman, says, "Honor is the greatest seed you can sow!"

> *Servants, obey in all things your masters according to the flesh; not with eyeservice, as menpleasers; but in singleness of heart, fearing God.*
> COLOSSIANS 3:22 KJV

EXCELLENCE

Most Christians are average. Very few are excellent. Excellence is doing something very good and to the best of your ability. Excellence is a choice; you were not born with it. Excellence is the privilege of a lifetime. Decide to wake up every day and choose to walk in excellence. To excel means to be first in rank, above average, beyond the norm. Excellence is pouring out and demonstrating your best with what you have. When you walk in excellence, you take ownership and 100% responsibility for your gifts and abilities.

Everything I do for my spiritual father must be done with excellence as unto the Lord. This distinguishes those who only do what they are

THE HEART OF A SON

told compared to those who go beyond by bringing excellence into their church and personal life. When I ask most people about what they are doing in their church or at work, most answer, "Just what they tell me to do." If I was your manager, I would fire you on the spot! The Kingdom of God is about honor and excellence in all we do. Go beyond what is asked of you and be sensitive to look for ways to display an excellent spirit into your workplace and church.

> *Whatever may be your task, work at it heartily (from the soul), as [something done] for the Lord and not for men.*
> COLOSSIANS 3:23 AMPC

> *Put your heart and soul into every activity you do, as though you are doing it for the Lord Himself and not merely for others.*
> COLOSSIANS 3:23 TPT

It's important to not just maintain what we have, but to increase what we have. My spiritual parents look each year in our leadership teams and members to upgrade! Upgrade is defined as raising something to a higher standard by adding or replacing components. In every church conference, in special events like a New Year's Eve dinner and service, in children's ministry and outreach, in Café after services, and more, we need to upgrade to a higher level of excellence as we execute these activities. My wife, Cindy, has the privilege to oversee some of these events in our church, and she spends hours researching ways to take these events to the next level. It's time to RANK UP! Read the parable of the talents in Matthew 25:14-30 to see this principle of increase.

Excellence is doing the little things nobody notices, like picking up trash from the floor, returning a grocery cart, or taking care of your personal responsibilities. You exude excellence when you live this way while no

PERFECTION OF SONS

one is watching. Excellence is showing up at work early and leaving late. In our church, we have taught our members to arrive at the meetings 15 minutes early so that you are ready to go at the start time. Somebody needs to lead the way with an excellent spirit to show our young people how to live it out. Be the example for those watching you.

I want to challenge you to walk in excellence as you grow as a leader. In our church, you can come as you are with no restrictions, but those of us in leadership walk in honor and excellence in our character, speech, dress, actions, and deeds because we are honoring the presence of God in the services. If a king or president walked into your church, you would not be wearing jeans with holes in them. You would come dressed for the occasion. SELAH. In this area, it's time to fear the Lord and His presence by bringing Him honor and excellence each time we come together with attitudes that convey this character quality of excellence.

Excellence will not tolerate unbelief, failure, procrastination, average, laziness, or the easy way out. Excellence is going the extra mile to do a better job than anyone else can do or has yet done. It is your ability to do it 100% with all your resources and skills. Don't leave anything behind as you do what God has assigned you to do. Excellence is vividly portrayed throughout the lives of the heroes and heroines in the pages of the Bible. Their lives reveal the evidence of the spirit of excellence.

> **EXCELLENCE IS YOUR ABILITY TO DO THINGS 100% WITH ALL YOUR RESOURCES AND SKILLS**

> *Then this Daniel was preferred above the presidents and princes, because an excellent spirit was in him; and the king thought to set him over the whole realm.*
> DANIEL 6:3 KJV

THE HEART OF A SON

And this I pray, that your love may abound yet more and more in knowledge and in all judgment; That ye may approve things that are excellent; that ye may be sincere and without offence till the day of Christ. Being filled with the fruits of righteousness, which are by Jesus Christ, unto the glory and praise of God.
PHILIPPIANS 1:9-11 KJV

So, these questions remain for us:

- What will you do today to make the choice to walk in a spirit of excellence?
- What do you need to change in your attitude, your actions, your dress, your thoughts, or your deeds to exhibit excellence?
- When people look at you, can they describe you as excellent? How does God rate you on a scale of 1-10 in the spirit of excellence?

Make the necessary changes, and step-by-step you will see excellence increase in your life.

SERVANTHOOD

A servant is one who performs duties to serve others. To serve means to give the service and respect due to (a superior) and to comply with the commands or demands of someone or something. It's easy to see entitlement in American culture. It means the feeling or belief that you deserve to be given something (such as special privileges).

But he that is greatest among you shall be your servant.
MATTHEW 23:11 KJV

PERFECTION OF SONS

To advance in God's Kingdom, you need to be a servant. I serve my spiritual father and mother in multiple ways. I know what their family enjoys. We not only serve in the church (my wife and I are honored to oversee multiple areas), but we also serve them with gifts throughout the year. If you love someone, you show them! They don't need any gifts, but I need to sow into their lives to show them honor and serve them.

> **TO ADVANCE IN GOD'S KINGDOM, YOU NEED TO BE A SERVANT**

We provide gift certificates to their favorite restaurants, stores where they like to shop, money on birthdays, holidays, Mother's and Father's Days, and a vacation fund to get away. You see, if I bless my set man and woman of God, it flows down on me (Psalms 133).

As I pour out blessings above me, the blessings of God pour down on my life. The reason why my entire seed line is blessed is because we are givers! We operate in the covenant of Abraham as heirs to that covenant.

> *And if you belong to Christ [are in Him Who is Abraham's Seed], then you are Abraham's offspring and [spiritual] heirs according to promise.*
> GALATIANS 3:29 AMPC

What promise is this referencing? The promise that we are blessed to be a blessing!

> *And I will make of thee a great nation, and I will bless thee, and make thy name great; and thou shalt be a blessing: And I will bless them that bless thee, and curse him that curseth thee: and in thee shall all families of the earth be blessed.*
> GENESIS 12:2-3 KJV

THE HEART OF A SON

I have never wanted for anything in my life! My living is based on my giving. When I stop giving, I stop living! We are out of debt because we help others get out of debt! We helped our children get out of debt, gave them a house, and bought them a new SUV. Why? God told us to bless our children and our children's children. You cannot outgive God, and it starts with your tithes, offerings, alms, and the seed of the increase from a raise or promotion. All of these types of giving go into the local church. It's also vital to include every year in your giving the first fruits that go directly to your spiritual father.

Serving can look different for everyone. Serve with your time, your talent, and your treasure. The most important aspect of being a servant is the ability to hear your Heavenly Father's voice so that you can best serve your spiritual parents and others that God directs you to. The heart of the servant is like Jesus when He washed His disciples' feet, healed the multitudes, taught His disciples the secrets of the Kingdom, and paid the ultimate price with His life through His death and resurrection. Begin serving today and watch the change it makes in your heart and life!

PRACTICAL FOCUS FOR PERFECTION

1. Honor begins in your mind with how you view others from God's perspective. Begin to develop an attitude of honoring someone close to you, such as family, your spiritual father, church leadership, friends, loved ones, or a boss/mentor.

    - What actions can you take to show honor to someone in your life this week?

PERFECTION OF SONS

2. You can start by addressing people by their title or saying "yes, ma'am" or yes, sir" when answering a specific question. If you begin to honor others, you will see how they will begin to honor you!

    - How will you explain to people this change you're making? Put it in your own words so you can share about honor with them.

    - How did people react when you spoke to them differently?

3. Take inventory of your personal conduct or behavior and identify the areas that you need to change.

    - Are there areas of dishonor that you can see in your life?

    - What needs to change?

4. Ask some close friends or relatives to help you identify a specific area where you can grow in excellence. You might be surprised at what you hear.

    - What did they say, and how did you take it?

    - How will you proceed to walk in excellence in these things?

THE HEART OF A SON

5. Look for ways to improve a situation every day by adding excellence to the mix.

   - Pick a situation in your life and make a list of how to add excellence to it in the ways you're involved.

   - What are the results?

CHAPTER FIVE
POSITION OF SONS

"Your position is your possession!"
DR. MARK KAUFFMAN

Jesus was a priest, prophet, king, and son. As He is, so are we in this world. If you are going to walk in sonship to both God the Father and to a spiritual father and mother, you must know your identity in Christ. Position is a state of being placed or the assignment of a person to a suitable place.

There are four key areas to understand your position in the Kingdom of God:

1. **Know who you are**—priest, prophet, king, and son

2. **Know what you have**—anointing, gifting, talents, acquired skills, capacity

3. **Know what to do with it and who needs it**—sphere of influence

4. **Know how to increase and develop it**—submission to authority, obedience, education

THE HEART OF A SON

PRIESTLY AND KINGLY ANOINTING

I want to begin this chapter by differentiating the priestly and kingly anointing on our lives. Most people operate in just their priestly anointing. As priests, we create vision, but as kings, we create provision through wealth transfer to advance the Kingdom. As priests, we are worshippers; as kings, we are warriors.

As a priest, we are empowered to worship, pray, and have an intimate relationship with the Lord Jesus Christ. Our priestly anointing also empowers us to minister to mankind, revealing God's love, mercy, and grace to all who are in need. Most people stop there. But we have evil principalities that are ruling in the 7 spheres of society – business, government, education, media, family, religion, arts and entertainment. Kings enter those spheres and release God's Kingdom, which all spheres are subject to in the earth.

> *The kingdoms of this world are become the kingdoms of our Lord, and of His Christ; and He shall reign for ever and ever.*
> REVELATION 11:15 KJV

We must also operate in our kingly anointing as a son of God. The kingly anointing gives you the power to rule and reign over your sphere of influence. To reign means to change things. Kings have the authority to transform lives, operate in dominion, rule over our enemies, and solve problems. The only way we will ever reach and control the 7 spheres of culture is with our kingly anointing. We are a military might, delivering creation from its present bondage. As kings, we are anointed to bring all enemies under our feet and bring a restraining order to every evil spirit. David operated both as king and priest and brought all his enemies under his feet! He is a true example of one who walked in these dual anointings. Look at the Pattern Son, Jesus, who also caused the enemy to leave after His time of fasting in the wilderness. Jesus wreaked havoc on hell, healing all who were oppressed by the devil. Incredible miracles flooded the earth through His ministry, and the Finished Work destroyed the works of the evil one.

SPHERES OF INFLUENCE

When I submitted myself to the apostolic counsel that became my spiritual covering, then my assignment became clear, and I experienced the release of manifestation in the calling on my life.

As a manager and trainer, God gave me the experiences needed to position me and place me into my destiny and purpose for what was to come after those roles! I created a 7 Vocational Spheres profile to help people get focused on their sphere of influence to positively invade and impact culture.

In 1975, Bill Bright, Loren Cunningham, and Francis Schaeffer were all given a similar message—if we are to impact any sphere of cultural influence, we ultimately must influence the seven vocational spheres, or mountains, that emerge as the pillars of any society. We have already identified these seven mountains as Education, Business, Arts and Entertainment, Media, Religion, Family/Social, and Government. Obviously, there are many subgroups under these main categories, but it is here where culture will be won or lost.

As a change-agent, what area will you focus on to influence society in a positive way? Where is your position in these 7 mountains of society? You can become the trend-setter by using your gifting and skill set in your specific mountain of influence to change the world! My spheres of influence are Business, Education, the Church, and recently, Government. My assignment is to raise up change-agents and provide them the resources to identify, quantify, and scale the sphere based on their gifting and skill set to positively influence society.

While we all have a responsibility to utilize our gifts, talents, and abilities to positively influence and change our culture, in over 45 years, we have not seen any change. Society does not yet resemble the Kingdom of God from the word the Lord gave these three great men.

One of the main reasons we have been ineffective here is that we send people out into these spheres before they have identified their apostolic covering. Without the proper order and government in place in their own lives, the result is confusion and lack of guidance. Another reason things have changed so little is because we are sending out untrained people; training both spiritually and naturally is lacking. Without apostolic and prophetic leaders decreeing and declaring over these strongholds and equipping individuals to enter their spheres, we will keep going around the mountains without seeing any change.

Dr. William Hinn, the spiritual father of my spiritual father, has a vision to equip students from a Kingdom perspective, and he is launching Kingdom of Christ University. There is a great need to be trained and educated before launching out. God is raising up seasoned leaders to do this.

> **LEADERS MUST BE TRAINED AND EDUCATED BEFORE BEING SENT OUT**

Under my spiritual father's vision, the Lord has called us to rise as leaders who bless our city. In 2012, Apostle Mark had a dream to feed the city. God showed him it was not a lack of food but a lack of money. God gave him the name to be the N.O.W. Project (Nourishing Others Well-being). We, as a church, began to prepare for this purpose to be fulfilled. Eight years later in March 2020, the world was impacted by the Covid-19 virus. It was time to move out as a wall-less church.

POSITION OF SONS

Everything started by us giving away bouquets of flowers to over 900 residents in our city's 8 local nursing homes. We then provided new board games to 450 families living in government-assisted apartments. The door then opened to feed those in need of food as we paid for 700 boxes of food in our first distribution. With the help of our local food bank and other suppliers, we began feeding over 4,000 families per month with multiple boxes of food.

In one of our food distributions, Pittsburgh Steelers quarterback Ben Roethlisberger and one of his Trucks of Hope traveled to the Shenango High School parking lot to work with the N.O.W. Project's effort, adding more items to the abundance of food we were already giving out to families. The Trucks of Hope chose New Castle because it is the hometown of Roethlisberger's wife, Ashley, a 2004 Laurel High School graduate. The joint distribution was sponsored by the Three Rivers Initiative, the Greater Pittsburgh Community Food Bank, and churches and ministries throughout the Pittsburgh area. Roethlisberger was joined by teammate Vance McDonald at the event in July.

Here is an article from the *New Castle News* that describes what we accomplished in just 15 months.

> *A pandemic-spawned initiative to provide food to local families continues to grow. The Nourishing Others' Well-being—or N.O.W.—Project was launched in the early days of the COVID-19 onslaught by Jubilee Ministries and the Christian Chamber of Commerce of Western Pennsylvania. At its first distribution at Cascade Park in May 2020, the initiative—led by Drs. Mark and Jill Kauffman of Jubilee—provided one box of food to each of 700 families.*

THE HEART OF A SON

It wasn't long before the distribution outgrew three venues and moved to the former Towne Mall, upping its provision count to between six and 10 boxes of food per family and serving thousands at one time instead of hundreds.

"At one point," Dr. Mark Kauffman said, "we had given away 15,000 boxes in one day. And what we've given away in retail, they've valued it at $13 million in 15 months." With the pandemic easing over the summer, the distribution has cut back to once a month, with around 400 families at each one. But that doesn't mean the N.O.W. Project has gone into cruise control. Instead, it has expanded into providing clothing, school supplies, and home goods as well.

"An opportunity came up where we were able to get brand new items from several box stores," Kauffman said. "These are returns they had, so they'd give them to us, and in turn, we give them to the community. We had our first distribution two weeks ago (at his church). The response was incredible. We gave away close to $65,000 worth of appliances, clothing, shoes, children's back-to-school items, office supplies—all brand new. We provided lunch for everybody; we had games for the kids. It was a really great day."

POSITION OF SONS

Our purpose is to fulfill the covenant of Abraham!

> *And if ye be Christ's, then are ye Abraham's seed, and heirs according to the promise.*
> GALATIANS 3:29 KJV

The promise outlined here is that we have been empowered to prosper to be a blessing!

> *And I will make of thee a great nation, and I will bless thee, and make thy name great; and thou shalt be a blessing: And I will bless them that bless thee, and curse him that curseth thee: and in thee shall all families of the earth be blessed.*
> GENESIS 12:2-3 KJV

Within 20 months of distributing food in our territory, we gave away $22 million worth of food, including meat, produce, dry goods, and milk. In addition, our Goods360 program is also providing household goods for local families. Your position as a son will always usher the Kingdom of God into the earth. People will be blessed because of your position as a son of God. Remember Joseph? After all, he endured from the pit to the prison, he ended up in the palace, but not just to sit ruling over others. He rose into his position to serve not only Egypt, but also other nations who came to them for provision. When his own family came, God restored all that was lost in his life. As you are in your position as a son, you can expect God to use your life to minister to others, and He will, in turn, minister to you as a Father who devotedly cares for His children. Your position will determine your destiny.

For me to equip the next generation, my daughter and my grandson, Joel (age 12 at the time), wanted to come and help distribute food. The local newspaper was there covering our food distribution, and the

THE HEART OF A SON

reporter came over and interviewed Joel about why he was there serving the people in the community. Here is a reprint of that article.

> *Joel Burnworth carried a heavy box of dried and canned food to a car Saturday morning, and after placing the crate in the car and before closing the door, he paused to say a prayer. Burnworth, 12, was one of about 40 volunteers in an assembly line who put food boxes into vehicles on Saturday as they drove through the county's free food distribution. It was his first time helping. Lawrence County was blessed to have an abundance of groceries to give to more than 500 families Saturday in the N.O.W. event—Nourishing Others' Well-being—sponsored by Jubilee Ministries International and the Christian Chamber of Commerce of Western Pennsylvania. The local event was coordinated by Jubilee minister Dr. Mark Kauffman. Jubilee Ministries is starting its third year of the massive distributions, which evolved from work shutdowns that resulted from COVID-19. The food was free to anyone in need, not only those who lost those jobs. Burnworth's parents and older church friends have been volunteering for the past several distributions, "and I felt like I was missing out," he said. "I didn't want to miss out on the fun."*
>
> NEW CASTLE NEWS MARCH 28, 2022

POSITION OF SONS

I have equipped my children at an early age to serve in the Kingdom, and now we are seeing our grandchildren serve the Lord at an early age under their spiritual father!

My son-in-law has also walked out this position as a son, and the Lord has shined favor in his life. He has received multiple raises and blessings at his job. He is a software engineer. When the plant he worked at was going to be closed, the mother office in Boston only retained about 10 employees from his office. He was the only one in his department that they wanted to retain. He has worked remotely with them and has had great compliments from his supervisors and co-workers. The revelation of your heart as a son impacts your assignment as you implement the truth of this position.

PRACTICAL FOCUS FOR POSITION

1. **Identify.** Do you know where you are called to effectively advance God's Kingdom in society?

    - Identify your spheres of influence where God can position and place you. You can take our profile at www.focuslifeinstitute.com with the Focus On Vocational Influence course.

2. **Find a mentor.** My prayer was answered when God brought me strategic relationships that I prayed for, and then I had to pursue them. It was up to me to go through the door God opened to these relationships. It is an investment of your time, and it costs you to submit yourself to these mentors as they speak into your life.

- List names of people in your life who are willing to mentor you as you grow into your position.

3. **Serve.** Become a servant leader in your local church under your spiritual father! Find a place to serve someone or in an activity that has a greater cause than yourself. Servant leadership is a great tool to position and place you into your destiny.

- Where will you begin serving this month and throughout this year?

CHAPTER SIX
PROCESS OF SONS

I define process as a series of actions or steps taken to achieve a particular end. Many people dislike the process! They want to go from A to Z and get their possession without going through the paces needed to get there. But remember to enjoy the journey and trust that God has it under control while you're walking through each step of the way.

For example, as a manager in Fortune 100, I would not have been able to even be selected to be interviewed by The Coca-Cola Company without a minimum of 10 years of experience. I gained this from working for Unilever—and this is just the world's system. So why do we think anything should be different in the Kingdom of God? Too many times, when we receive a prophetic word or revelation in the Word of God, we think, "Presto, I can walk in this right now." But this is not God's order. While I believe God does accelerate the time, there are still prophetic words I received over 25 years ago that I am still believing for to happen! Don't give in or give up! God is working His nature in us to prepare us to handle our specific end to faithfully fulfill our assignment and destiny.

THE HEART OF A SON

I can tell you from experience that walking through the process is not easy. Many quit, become frustrated, take offense, and even leave the call of God upon their lives. STAY THE COURSE! Offenses will come and go, but in the Kingdom, you need to develop, mature, grow a tough skin, and humble yourself. Watch God lift you up when you stay the course. Many people have lived for decades in the Kingdom only to quit at the last minute. This breaks my heart because not only do they quit, but they break covenant relationships.

When the Lord spoke to me to leave my denominational church, I left properly. I left with a blessing and was a sent one to my next step in my process. When you are not a "sent one," you are a "went one" without the blessing. During this part of our process, God was lifting my wife, children, and me into a higher level of revelation in every move that He asked us to make. In this specific example, there are many times people will not leave a local church. Instead, they believe they are going to change the pastor to go to a higher level of revelation. This will never happen in this order, and they waste years by remaining stagnant like a hamster on a wheel. By leaving in order, they could have saved everyone's time and energy by going to the next level of revelation to find their assignment and purpose in life.

One of the greatest lessons we learn in the process is our ability to submit to a higher authority!

> *And if ye have not been faithful in that which is another*
> *man's, who shall give you that which is your own?*
> LUKE 16:12 KJV

Yes, learn to submit to the leaders God places in your life: a set man/woman of God, a boss, manager, and leader of a group/organization. If you cannot submit to a man that God has placed before you, how are you going to submit to God Whom you cannot see? This is the greatest problem I have experienced with many individuals. The result is that they miss the call of God. This stems from an independent spirit within them that does not want to be told what to do. The Scriptures expound on how to rid yourself of an independent spirit through the power of submission:

> *Submit yourselves for the LORD's sake to every human authority: whether to the emperor, as the supreme authority.*
> 1 PETER 2:13 NIV

> *Submit to one another out of reverence for Christ.*
> EPHESIANS 5:21 KJV

> *Let everyone be subject to the governing authorities, for there is no authority except that which God has established. The authorities that exist have been established by God.*
> ROMANS 13:1 NIV

> *Have confidence in your leaders and submit to their authority, because they keep watch over you as those who must give an account. Do this so that their work will be a joy, not a burden, for that would be of no benefit to you.*
> HEBREWS 13:17 NIV

As a church leader for over 40 years, I have seen great, anointed men and women forsake the call of God on their life because they either became offended or would not obey their set man or woman of God and CHANGE! Apostolic ministries and apostles will demand us to CHANGE! The goal is a transformed life by an intimate relationship with God and revelation of truth from His Word.

The message of the Kingdom will offend you, convict you, challenge you, and FORCE you to change! While I was praying one day, the Lord showed

THE HEART OF A SON

me a picture of a person representing one who needed to be redeemed. His clothes were stained and dirty. As a few of us were ministering to him, asking God to wash and cleanse him, the Lord directed me to look at my clothes. He said, "Your clothes are not stained, but there is some residue of the flesh that still needs to be brushed off!"

I quickly repented and asked God to cleanse me of my fleshly, selfish nature. I do not want any residue (a small amount of something that remains after the main part has gone or been taken or used) on me. Even a small amount taints the whole. God cleanses every detail of our lives.

> *But I say, walk and live [habitually] in the [Holy] Spirit*
> *[responsive to and controlled and guided by the Spirit];*
> *then you will certainly not gratify the cravings and*
> *desires of the flesh (of human nature without God).*
> GALATIANS 5:16 AMPC

I love this version of Paul's letter to the Galatians. We must be responsive to the small, still voice of the Holy Spirit. We must let Him control our thoughts, words, deeds, and actions. We must be guided by the Holy Spirit so we do not fulfill the lust or desires of our flesh.

I have seen the same issue in businesses in the marketplace. Many people will not submit to a leader or manager; they get offended and walk out. Thirty years later, they have no retirement, pension, or 401K, and their limited experiences show for their efforts. Or they work for another company and cause the same friction and strife wherever they go. The pattern continues no matter where they end up in life. If you want to see blessings in your life, then study the Word about submission. By doing so, you will learn to submit to the process and the individuals God has brought your way. You will change, enter His fullness, and enjoy deeper experiences with the Lord when you value the principle of submission.

PROCESS OF SONS

My process began when I decided to move to the next level of revelation, be baptized in the Holy Ghost, and walk in the Spirit. I am still walking through the process of God perfecting (maturing) me to advance His Kingdom. During the years between 1989 – 1992, I received many prophetic words of how God would use me in business and ministry. What followed were several processes I needed to walk through to achieve my assignment, purpose, and destiny.

> YOU WILL NEED TO EMBRACE THE PROCESS TO ACHIEVE YOUR ASSIGNMENT, PURPOSE, AND DESTINY

Each process causes you to progress so that each time you cycle through God's maturation, the results of the process become infinitely greater. After several years of growth, I realized I would need to embrace the culture of an apostolic church under the leadership of an apostle who incorporated the 5-fold ministry gifts. This was different from my previous churches that operated in the pastoral paradigm. This is the biggest cultural change that most people do not understand yet, and it takes time to embrace it.

After 25 years of ministry experience, I realized how we had to embrace the new Kingdom wineskin when my wife and I were called to our current church in 2008. We were invited to our first leadership meeting and learned that we had come there to join them, not to change them. What we had experienced in our past churches would not work here because, as a Kingdom church, we have never been this way before. There is no roadmap or model to follow. We are pioneers advancing the Kingdom of God. What even worked last year will not work this year. Most churches just maintain what they know, but Kingdom churches are forerunners to establish a new creation reality. This reality is the sons of God, a military might, delivering creation from its present bondage.

THE HEART OF A SON

Let's look at a biblical example about the process that Timothy walked out under his spiritual father, the Apostle Paul. The Apostle Paul was a spiritual father to Timothy and Titus, as well as others who were born again under his ministry. Spiritual fathers are a scriptural pattern in the Word for us to model today.

> *For though ye have ten thousand instructors in Christ, yet have ye not many fathers: for in Christ Jesus I have begotten you through the Gospel.*
> 1 CORINTHIANS 4:15 KJV

Timothy's name means honoring God. Honor is one of the greatest virtues in the Kingdom of God and Timothy honored both God and the man that God placed in his life as his spiritual father.

> *And [Paul] went down to Derbe and also to Lystra. A disciple named Timothy was there, the son of a Jewish woman who was a believer [she had become convinced that Jesus is the Messiah and the Author of eternal salvation, and yielded obedience to Him]; but [Timothy's] father was a Greek. He [Timothy] had a good reputation among the brethren at Lystra and Iconium. Paul desired Timothy to go with him [as a missionary]; and he took him and circumcised him because of the Jews that were in those places, all of whom knew that his father was a Greek.*
> ACTS 16:1-3 AMPC

Timothy had to submit to Paul's request to be circumcised. His was a mature response to the request of his father. We can learn from this example as a metaphor in our relationships with our spiritual fathers today. There are times when your spiritual father must circumcise your

PROCESS OF SONS

flesh, or deal with your selfish actions. He will either request it of you or you can bring the knife to your father, allowing him to speak into your life to produce CHANGE! As time progressed in Paul and Timothy's lives, Timothy became known for his good reputation (good name and character) in the territory where he ministered. God is moving in this day and hour to build our character. What is your character like? It is no longer about your gifting alone, but how you couple your anointing with character.

> *Paul, an apostle of Jesus Christ, by the commandment of God our Savior and the Lord Jesus Christ, our hope, To Timothy, a true son in the faith: Grace, mercy, and peace from God our Father and Jesus Christ our Lord.*
>
> 1 TIMOTHY 1:1 NKJV

Paul calls Timothy a true son. According to *Webster's 1828 Dictionary*, the word true means genuine, pure, real; not counterfeit, adulterated, or false. It also means faithful; steady in adhering to promises, to someone in a position over you.

As a son to your spiritual father, you need to be faithful, steady, and loyal. Loyalty is royalty in the Kingdom of God! Many people take offense from their spiritual father when they receive correction. They become upset and leave their ministry with the excuse that "God" told them to leave. But the right response to correction is to say thank you and watch the change happen in your life. See the ways God will increase you by the instruction and guidance from your spiritual father. If you have difficulty taking correction and receiving instruction, something is out of order in your life. Start to change your perspective and the attitude of your heart. See that your father is trying to help you grow; your refusal will cause you to miss your destiny because of an offense.

THE HEART OF A SON

*This charge (command) I commit to you, son Timothy,
according to the prophecies previously made
concerning you, that by them you may wage the good
warfare, having faith and a good conscience.*
1 TIMOTHY 1:18-19A NKJV

Apostle Paul, his spiritual father, is giving him the process to mature in the Kingdom. It is a command and a charge! As true sons, we wage good warfare by meditating on our prophetic words, and we war by declaring them to come to pass.

*You shall also decide and decree a thing, and
it shall be established for you; and the light [of
God's favor] shall shine upon your ways.*
JOB 22:28 AMPC

By decreeing your prophetic promises over your life in faith with a good conscience (defined as the faculty, power, or principle within us), you mature to enter your calling and assignment. Our words have authority when we are under the authority of our spiritual parents.

*For this very cause I sent to you Timothy, who is my
beloved and trustworthy child in the Lord, who will
recall to your minds my methods of proceeding and
course of conduct and way of life in Christ, such as
I teach everywhere in each of the churches.*
1 CORINTHIANS 4:17 AMPC

Timothy was sent with his spiritual father's message. When you come under your set man and woman of God, you will be able to take their revelation into the minds and hearts of others, producing the life

PROCESS OF SONS

of Christ. Who you hang out with is who you become! What you are receiving, you will be able to effectively live out and impart to those under your influence.

> *When Timothy arrives, see to it that [you put him at ease, so that] he may be fearless among you, for he is [devotedly] doing the Lord's work, just as I am.*
> 1 CORINTHIANS 16:10 TPT

Timothy was a son who replicated his father. As a spiritual son to my father, I will do the Lord's work just as my father does. I am not the set man; I am a spiritual son under the set man. This is probably the hardest position in an apostolic ministry because you must honor, submit, and serve the first family. Your ego must be set aside. I must decrease, and God must increase in me. If you serve this man's vision, you will reap in your own destiny and assignment! This is God's way and order. You serve your way into your destiny.

> *But Timothy's tested worth you know, how as a son with his father he has toiled with me zealously in [serving and helping to advance] the good news (the Gospel).*
> PHILIPPIANS 2:22 AMPC

Here we have that "dirty word" called WORK! The word toil is described in *Webster's 1828 Dictionary* as: labor, to work, to exert strength with pain and fatigue of body or mind. Zealously means with passionate ardor and eagerness to pursue. To fulfill what God has given your set man, your spiritual father, means going to work to serve the vision. It is focusing your time, talent, and treasure to advance the Kingdom of God.

Sons are purposed for assignments.

THE HEART OF A SON

> *And we sent Timothy, our brother and God's servant in [spreading] the good news (the Gospel) of Christ, to strengthen and establish and to exhort and comfort and encourage you in your faith.*
> 1 THESSALONIANS 3:2 AMPC

Timothy's assignment was to build up the faith of the church and minister to the Body of Christ in the regions where Paul sent him. The Lord spoke to me many years ago about this Scripture in Acts regarding what sons are called to do to support their spiritual fathers.

> *Establishing and strengthening the souls and the hearts of the disciples, urging and warning and encouraging them to stand firm in the faith, and [telling them] that it is through many hardships and tribulations we must enter the Kingdom of God.*
> ACTS 14:22 AMPC

If you are going to be a true son who is covered by a spiritual father/set man and ready to advance the Kingdom, then expect hardship, trials, and tribulations. Yet, know God will deliver you out of them all!

> *O Timothy, guard and keep the deposit entrusted [to you]! Turn away from the irreverent babble and godless chatter, with the vain and empty and worldly phrases, and the subtleties and the contradictions in what is falsely called knowledge and spiritual illumination.*
> 1 TIMOTHY 6:20 AMPC

Paul's direction to Timothy here is specific and critical to his success. As a true son, you must stay FOCUSED! There will be many who will tell you

PROCESS OF SONS

that your spiritual father is controlling and manipulative. However, learn to discern and examine your spiritual covering by these standards: true apostolic fathers want their sons to go higher, exceed them, and cover them in their day of battle. I have been under both true and false fathers. By discernment and prayer, I was able to identify my true spiritual father.

A spiritual father's main objective is to build Christ in you! To do that, you must CHANGE and mature in the Lord. There will be many who will start the process of submitting to a spiritual father, but because they refuse to CHANGE, they will leave and blame their father. As Paul tells Timothy, guard what has been entrusted to you! You cannot become familiar with your spiritual father or mother. Be thankful for them and train yourself not to speak against them. God has issued the anointing and call upon their life, and we must understand their position in the Kingdom.

> **A SPIRITUAL FATHER'S MAIN OBJECTIVE IS TO BUILD CHRIST IN YOU**

> *Notice that our brother Timothy has been released [from prison]. If he comes here soon, I will see you along with him.*
> HEBREWS 13:23 AMPC

As you submit to a spiritual father, just make sure you know that whatever he endures and suffers, you will also go through. Just as Paul went to prison, Timothy encountered the same situation. However, I have good news! Similarly, the anointing flows down, so in this process, all the blessings that your spiritual father receives, you will obtain the same blessings.

If you want to learn how to operate with the heart of a son, the following verses of the life of Timothy provide the principles and patterns of what the apostle calls a true and beloved son.

THE HEART OF A SON

But you, Timothy, have closely followed my example and the truth that I've imparted to you. You have modeled your life after the love and endurance I've demonstrated in my ministry by not giving up.

The faith I have, you now have. What I have hungered for in life has now become your longing as well. The patience I have with others, you now demonstrate. And the same persecutions and difficulties I have endured, you have also endured.

Yes, you know all about what I had to suffer while in Antioch, Iconium, and Lystra. You're aware of all the persecution I endured there; yet the Lord delivered me from every single one of them! For all who choose to live godly as worshipers of Jesus, the Anointed One, will also experience persecution.

But the evil men and sorcerers will progress from bad to worse, deceived and deceiving, as they lead people further from the truth. Yet you must continue to advance in strength with the truth wrapped around your heart, being assured by God that he's the One who has truly taught you all these things.

Remember what you were taught from your childhood from the Holy Scrolls which can impart to you wisdom to experience everlasting life through the faith of Jesus, the Anointed One! God has transmitted his very substance into every Scripture, for it is God-breathed.

PROCESS OF SONS

It will empower you by its instruction and correction, giving you the strength to take the right direction and lead you deeper into the path of godliness. Then you will be God's servant, fully mature and perfectly prepared to fulfill any assignment God gives you.
2 TIMOTHY 3:10-17 TPT

Let's review this pattern of true sonship!

- He followed his spiritual father's example, living out the truth that was imparted to him.
- He modeled his life after the love and endurance that the Apostle Paul demonstrated and never gave up, modeling an attitude of perseverance.
- He received what his father had: Paul's faith, you now have. "What I have hungered for in life has now become your longing as well. The patience I have with others, you now demonstrate."
- He suffered and endured the same persecutions and difficulties as Paul, but God delivered Timothy like He delivered Paul.
- He would continue to advance the Kingdom message in strength with the truth wrapped around his heart.
- He was able to come into maturity by the power of God's Word as God's servant, fully mature and perfectly prepared to fulfill any assignment God gave him.

Do you want to be prepared to fulfill any assignment God gives you? Then glean from your spiritual father! Timothy became like his spiritual father, and we can see the results. Psalm 133 (KJV) became a reality in Timothy's life.

THE HEART OF A SON

Behold, how good and how pleasant it is for brethren to dwell together in unity! It is like the precious ointment upon the head, that ran down upon the beard, even Aaron's beard: that went down to the skirts of his garments; As the dew of Hermon, and as the dew that descended upon the mountains of Zion: for there the Lord commanded the blessing, even life for evermore.

The anointing flows down from the head (your spiritual father) down to you. It does not flow up. So, as you submit yourself in this process, God will command the blessing into your life!

The following Scriptures are a reminder of what we need to do as sons of God. Paul encouraged Timothy in the following Scriptures. As a son, we need to be attentive to these types of encouragements from our spiritual father.

- **Wage a good warfare of your faith!**

    This charge and admonition I commit in trust to you, Timothy, my son, in accordance with prophetic intimations which I formerly received concerning you, so that inspired and aided by them you may wage the good warfare, Holding fast to faith (that leaning of the entire human personality on God in absolute trust and confidence) and having a good (clear) conscience. By rejecting and thrusting from them [their conscience], some individuals have made shipwreck of their faith.

    1 TIMOTHY 1:18-19 AMPC

PROCESS OF SONS

- **Stir up and fan the flame of the gift of God in you!** Timothy had some fear, but true sons can overcome fear and walk in power, love, and a sound mind!

    That is why I would remind you to stir up (rekindle the embers of, fan the flame of, and keep burning) the [gracious] gift of God, [the inner fire] that is in you by means of the laying on of my hands [with those of the elders at your ordination]. For God did not give us a spirit of timidity (of cowardice, of craven and cringing and fawning fear), but [He has given us a spirit] of power and of love and of calm and well-balanced mind and discipline and self-control.

    2 TIMOTHY 1:6-7 AMPC

- **Study the Word daily!**

    Study and be eager and do your utmost to present yourself to God approved (tested by trial), a workman who has no cause to be ashamed, correctly analyzing and accurately dividing [rightly handling and skillfully teaching] the Word of Truth.

    2 TIMOTHY 2:15 AMPC

THE HEART OF A SON

PRACTICAL FOCUS FOR PROCESS

1. Embrace the journey of the process with joy and thanksgiving. God knows what He is doing and will bring you through!

    - Write down at least five things you are thankful for! Keep a thankful heart always.

2. Each process brings you to a new level of maturity!

    I am convinced and confident of this very thing, that He who has begun a good work in you will [continue to] perfect and complete it until the day of Christ Jesus [the time of His return].
    PHILIPPIANS 1:6 AMP

    - Describe a time when you went through a processing time that matured you and accelerated your growth.

3. Identify the how and where the process of God is changing you. Sometimes it comes down to that one weakness, that one thing that continually stops the process of being completed. Make time with the Lord today and ask God for the strategy to walk through the process.

    - List two areas where you need to change and write down the strategies the Lord gives you to overcome them.

PROCESS OF SONS

4. There will constantly be trials and tribulations as a Kingdom person. However, God has promised to walk you through each of these processes of maturity to perfect you in your life.

   Establishing and strengthening the souls and the hearts of the disciples, urging and warning and encouraging them to stand firm in the faith, and [telling them] that it is through many hardships and tribulations we must enter the Kingdom of God.
   ACTS 14:22 AMPC

- Testify of a time when this has happened or write a declaration of this truth regarding a difficult situation in your life right now.

THE HEART OF A SON

WHEN YOU SUBMIT YOURSELF TO PROCESS, GOD WILL COMMAND BLESSING INTO YOUR LIFE!

CHAPTER SEVEN
PROPHETIC OF SONS

This is a truth that I have learned through many great experiences from the prophetic realm. Coming out of a denomination church in the 1980s, we had never heard of the prophetic. But that night in August 1988, when the word was spoken over our lives, it ignited our spirits into the truth of the Kingdom.

Before this experience, we knew there was more, but without obeying the prompting of the Holy Spirit to visit that church on that specific weekend, we would have never been able to begin the process to fulfill our assignment in the earth.

Over the last 30-plus years, we have received many confirming prophetic words over our lives. The more you mature in the Kingdom, the fewer words you will receive; if you do get a prophetic word, it is confirmation of what God already spoke to you in His presence in the quiet place. That is why a presence driven life is the most important FOCUS you must maintain daily. As you grow in the Lord, you become your best prophet.

THE HEART OF A SON

It is critical in these days that the prophetic is accurate. As prophetic people, we understand the times where we live and what we are to do in this season.

> *And of the children of Issachar, which were men that had understanding of the times, to know what Israel ought to do; the heads of them were two hundred; and all their brethren were at their commandment.*
> 1 CHRONICLES 12:32 KJV

It is important to understand how the prophetic operates and how the Word of God explains the prophetic realm for us:

> *Everyone should be trained how to prophesy! That does not mean your specific calling is to be a prophet, but you can grow as a prophetic person. For ye may all prophesy one by one, that all may learn, and all may be comforted.*
> 1 CORINTHIANS 14:31 KJV

When you receive a prophetic word, it will be tested! I can assure you that every word we have ever received has been tested!

> *He sent a man before them, even Joseph, who was sold for a servant: Whose feet they hurt with fetters: he was laid in iron: Until the time that his word came: the word of the Lord tried him.*
> PSALM 105:17-19 KJV

When you receive a prophetic word, you must know it is speaking of your potential and future. **It will always be a positive word over your life, but you must *believe*** that the word spoken will prosper your life. God plans what is best for you.

PROPHETIC OF SONS

Believe in the LORD your God, so shall ye be established;
believe His prophets, so shall ye prosper.
2 CHRONICLES 20:20B KJV

When God gives you a word for someone in the church, you should always have a leader present before you speak the word to judge it. If you are out in public, make sure the word you receive is a word from God and not your flesh. Many people have been hurt from a "prophetic word" that is not given in order; it can become what we call "parking lot prophecies" because the person is not submitted to authority. They sneak in their prophecies in the parking lot away from their covering/leadership. If you get a word for someone, it can wait until you have a leader present. True submission looks like this: when God gives me a word during a service, I submit that word to the set man or woman and then let them determine if the word should be given or not. Once I submit it to my leaders, I am now free because the word is released in the hands of leadership, and they follow God's leading regarding it.

Let all things be done decently and in order.
1 CORINTHIANS 14:40 KJV

The prophetic word is a light to you, and you need to write down your prophetic word, pray over it, listen to it if it was recorded, and submit it to leadership who will have insight for this word to come to pass.

And so we have the prophetic word confirmed, which you
do well to heed as a light that shines in a dark place, until
the day dawns and the morning star rises in your hearts.
2 PETER 1:19 NKJV

As you spend time in God's presence, be open to the prophetic and allow it to confirm what the Lord has already spoken to you. Please

THE HEART OF A SON

remember that you need the apostles and prophets for the Kingdom to effectively work in your life.

> *And are built upon the foundation of the apostles and prophets, Jesus Christ Himself being the Chief Cornerstone.*
> EPHESIANS 2:20 KJV

When the apostolic and prophetic converge, you will see the church arise to a new level. Prophets can prophesy what is going to happen, and the apostles will provide the blueprint to build and see the prophetic word come to pass.

As Paul told his son Timothy, you must also war over your prophecies. It is one thing to write them out and get counsel, but I have over 100 pages of prophecies regarding my life, family, children, and business! Yet, I must war over these by putting God in remembrance of His Word over me and my family (see Isaiah 43:26).

> *So, Timothy, my son, I am entrusting you with this responsibility, in keeping with the very first prophecies that were spoken over your life and are now in the process of fulfillment in this great work of ministry, in keeping with the prophecies spoken over you. With this encouragement use your prophecies as weapons as you wage spiritual warfare by faith and with a clean conscience.*
> 1 TIMOTHY 1:18 TPT

Each of us needs to FOCUS and spend time declaring our prophetic words (Job 22:28). Heed these words from the Apostle Peter:

> *And so we have been given the prophetic word—the written message of the prophets, made more reliable*

PROPHETIC OF SONS

and fully validated by the confirming voice of God on the Mount of Transfiguration. And you will continue to do well if you stay focused on it. For this prophetic message is like a piercing light shining in a gloomy place until the dawning of a new day, when the Morning Star rises in your hearts. You must understand this at the outset: Interpretation of scriptural prophecy requires the Holy Spirit, for it does not originate from someone's own imagination. No true prophecy comes from human initiative but is inspired by the moving of the Holy Spirit upon those who spoke the message that came from God.
2 PETER 1:19-21 TPT

Recently, we held special prayer meetings every night at our church for a week. My three grandchildren attended, participated in the prayer time, and even prayed prophetic decrees during the meeting. They were very excited to be part of these services. During one of the services, Drs. Mark and Jill Kauffman prophesied over the three of them together. They paralleled the three of them to Moses, Aaron, and Miriam. By the time the three of them turn 16, Apostle Mark declared that they would be flowing in the gift of prophecy, and the Lord had plans to use them in ministry together like Moses, Aaron, and Miriam. Apostle Jill encouraged them regarding their relationship, explaining how the Lord has intertwined them together. Nothing will be able to break them apart. One word from God has changed their lives forever! Now, they are expecting more prophetic experiences in their lives and are studying this prophetic word with their parents. Spiritual parents pour into their spiritual sons and stir up the prophetic. As you submit to your covering, expect the Lord to use you more in the prophetic gifts.

THE HEART OF A SON

PRACTICAL FOCUS FOR PROPHETIC

1. One word from God can change your entire life from a true prophet! Here is the process I follow when I get a prophetic word:

   - Write it out word for word and keep a copy in a prophetic word notebook.

   - Use Scripture to validate it. The prophetic word needs to be backed by the Word of God. Begin to meditate on it and decree it. Begin to declare these prophetic promises over your life every day in faith to see the manifestation (see Job 22:28).

   - Did it bring confirmation to you? Most of the prophetic words I get are a direct confirmation of what God has been speaking to me when I am spending time in an intimate relationship with Him. It confirms the things I have written in my personal journal.

     We have also a more sure word of prophecy; whereunto ye do well that ye take heed, as unto a light that shineth in a dark place, until the day dawn, and the day star arise in your hearts.
     2 PETER 1:19 KJV

   - I always bring the prophetic word to my spiritual covering to provide counsel and direction. I have seen many people miss the plan of God and its timing because they refused to acquire counsel from their spiritual covering.

     Where no counsel is, the people fall: but in the multitude of counsellors there is safety.
     PROVERBS 11:14 KJV

PROPHETIC OF SONS

- Each prophetic word is conditional. I must be living a life in the Spirit and be in prayer, obedience, and intimacy with God.

- You must know the timing of God. There are seasons when God is moving, and manifestation is upon you. Don't negate the preparation process to position you for this prophetic word to come to pass.

    He hath made everything beautiful in His time.
    ECCLESIASTES 3:11A KJV

- There is a time to pray and a time to say (remember Job 22:28). You must declare and decree over these prophetic words out of your mouth in faith. You cannot keep silent and think it will come to pass! In *The Focus Fulfilled Life* book and workbook, I teach my plan for 40 Days of Focus. Focusing on 1-2 things for the next 40 days and using Scriptures to back them up has produced tremendous manifestations to those who have utilized the 40 Days of Focus.[1]

2. Now that you have reviewed my process, list the process that you want to implement when you receive a word from the Lord.

ENDNOTES

1 For more on the 40 Days of Focus, read *The Focus Fulfilled Life: Experience the Power of FOCUS and Get Results!* Available on **amazon.com**.

THE HEART OF A SON

ONE WORD FROM GOD CAN CHANGE YOUR LIFE FOREVER!

CHAPTER EIGHT
PLAN OF SONS

A plan is a method for achieving a desired end. Why would God want to bless us financially if we do not have a plan to advance His Kingdom on the earth? Jesus was supplied with everything He needed because He had a plan. Jesus had a plan to go to multiple cities. He had a plan when He taught about the Kingdom. Jesus' plan was also evident in His death, resurrection, and ascension.

> *Pilate therefore said unto him, "Art thou a king then?"*
> *Jesus answered, "Thou sayest that I am a king. To*
> *this end was I born, and for this cause came I into*
> *the world, that I should bear witness unto the truth.*
> *Every one that is of the truth heareth My voice."*
> JOHN 18:37 KJV

Jesus' plan was to establish His Kingdom on the earth through His sons (male and female).

> *There is neither Jew nor Greek, there is neither bond nor free,*
> *there is neither male nor female: for ye are all one in Christ Jesus.*
> GALATIANS 3:28 KJV

THE HEART OF A SON

It's exciting to see the plan of God unfold in your lives, even from generation to generation. This also correlates to families who have had spiritual covering over the years. My parents and my wife's parents were the first of their families to faithfully commit to their churches and seek the Lord consistently. My wife and I increased in our journey with the Lord and experienced more of the things of God than they had because they paved the way for us to do so. As you have read, we received the baptism of the Holy Ghost and the gifts of the Spirit, then moving into the apostolic and prophetic in a deeper way. We have come into submission as sons to our spiritual father and mother.

Our children have built upon our foundation. They both experienced salvation at a young age, served in our church, have never departed from the faith, and learned of the power of the Holy Spirit operative in their lives even during childhood. They witnessed miracles and the powerful presence of God for all their lives! Our grandchildren, now the fourth generation, are born of Zion, and know nothing else, immersed in the Kingdom of God. They pursue God passionately, praise Him wholeheartedly, serve in church, and understand apostolic covering. They honor their spiritual parents and have had this relationship with them since birth. All were dedicated by their current spiritual covering and are launching into deep waters even now. They are 13 years and under at the writing of this book. Our journey testifies to God's powerful plan of sonship with a spiritual father and mother. It is priceless!

> **TO BE EFFECTIVE, YOU NEED A PLAN FOR YOUR LIFE**

To be effective, you need a plan for your life, and God will allow that plan to be submitted to your apostolic covering for it to happen. The greatest process for your life is to have an action plan and follow it. This plan comes from your intimate time with God. When I was downsized in 1995, I entered a time of fasting and prayer about what

PLAN OF SONS

I was supposed to do next. I invested in myself and became a certified behavioral consultant with the DISC behavioral system using it in my church and local businesses.

The Lord showed me that I should train and change generations by taking the DISC system into schools. I took this idea to a Christian business owner that I knew, and he decided to embrace the idea to market a student program called Career Quest. I worked and created some of the six workbooks of the program, selling this to colleges and schools. However, promises were made to me and never kept. You must understand that this was my assignment and not his, so it did not work at the level I had expected. After three years, I received a prophetic word that there would be a repositioning in my career. Coca-Cola called me back and gave me my entire eight years of tenure back to me.

I thought my plan was with this business owner, but God had a better plan for me. I sowed this idea of the Career Quest program and walked away. Fifteen years later, God told me this was my assignment and to pick it up again with His blessing on it. I was thankful for the three years I spent under this man as I learned a lot from him, but God had a plan that was greater in this educational arena than what this business owner was called to do in that field. You see, I blessed him with this idea, and he prospered in it, but it was only a 30-fold plan when God wanted me to have the 100-fold plan.

For years I would confess and decree the anointings associated with the Spirit of the Lord as described by Isaiah.

> *And the spirit of the Lord shall rest upon him, the spirit of wisdom and understanding, the spirit of counsel and might, the spirit of knowledge and of the fear of the Lord.*
> ISAIAH 11:2 KJV

THE HEART OF A SON

I needed the anointing of the Spirit of the Lord if I was going to train and change generations! The prophetic words over the Focus Life Institute declare that we will bring hope to the hopeless by providing the skills they need to advance in the workplace through the values and character development necessary for success.

Once I received the Word from the Lord, it was now time to work on the plan. As I created online courses, His grace (divine enablement) showed up. I gathered a few of my like-minded, gifted friends, and they helped me create multiple courses to launch the Focus Life Institute. I retired from Coca-Cola in 2017, freeing up more time to focus on this venture. There have been many tweaks along the way in the development since I have retired and embraced this full-time, but I continue to follow God's plan with consistency to achieve His plan for this program.

I want to emphasize that this plan was the assignment God wanted me to follow. Remember, an assignment is an undertaking or duty that you have been assigned to perform or accomplish. Everything I do must align with my assignment. Once I detailed my plan, I realized how it fit into my spiritual covering's plan and vision where I am faithful and serve. God has orchestrated a perfect union for my assignment to match the vision of my apostolic covering.

You must lay down your plan and your agenda for the greater cause of how your vision can advance the Kingdom of God. Focus Life Institute is being used to equip and train individuals to FOCUS on their assignment that will help advance the Kingdom. We offer online courses for personal growth, professional development (marketplace training), K-12 curriculum (club classes, electives, or entire curriculum), college retention and workplace preparation courses, recovery and re-entry courses for those being released back into society. We provide a 7-sphere vocational profile that identifies your placement and position

PLAN OF SONS

so you can be equipped to enter your mountain in your city and sphere of influence where God has placed over you with your spiritual covering. As time has progressed, our materials have and will be utilized even more in multiple areas based on the vision that my spiritual father has for the city. People who have had no hope or vision for their lives will have the tools to discover their divine destinies in Christ, and that is so fulfilling! God's plan is truly greater than we can imagine!

PRACTICAL FOCUS FOR PLAN

1. Spend time in God's presence to get His plan. Listen and write down what He says. Follow it by being Holy Spirit led.

   - What is He speaking to you today? How will you execute it?

2. Identify how your vision and plan will be submitted and utilized under the plan of your spiritual covering. Meet with your church leaders and/or spiritual parents to discuss this with them. Take notes with their insights.

   - Write a reflection of this experience and include action steps to move forward.

3. Does your plan advance the Kingdom for His glory? If not, you need to get into the quiet place and see how God wants to use your plan and gifting.

- How does this plan point to Christ? How does it lead people into the truth of the Word of God? How does it reveal the principles of God's Kingdom?

4. For your plan to work properly, it needs to come under your spiritual covering. For example, my plan for the Focus Life Institute fits into what we are called to do through my church/spiritual covering locally, in the United States, and nations around the world.

- Detail your plan and submit a copy in brief to your spiritual covering for their prayer and agreement with what the Lord has shown you.

CHAPTER NINE
PRINCIPLES OF SONS

In the Kingdom, we live by principles and patterns. My apostle has been a role model in operating by these Kingdom standards. At my church, Jubilee Ministries International, our culture is one of honor, excellence, and servanthood. These three cultural values are applied in everything we do. Prophets and apostles who come to visit us tell us they have never seen anything like this before! We are operating in these values and character traits that set us apart from many churches/organizations. Our decision to corporately walk in these areas produces great fruit for the Kingdom.

Society, in general, has lost these valuable principles that need to be re-established in our personal and professional arenas. If you can begin to focus on and incorporate these into your life, you will see great favor and success. In chapter 2, I detailed these powerful principles that impact how we live our lives: honor, excellence, responsibility, order, expectation, and servanthood. If you are going to operate in the Kingdom, you will need to incorporate these 6 key HEROES principles every day. In my HEROES

THE HEART OF A SON

books, I have included a HEROES profile with a series of questions about each one of these principles so you can examine yourself to see where you need to improve to advance the Kingdom.

When I retired from the Coca-Cola Company in 2017, my boss flew my wife and me to Orlando, Florida, for my retirement party. In my final meeting with all my peers, my boss had me train the employees in the HEROES Effect principles. I received a standing ovation because of what was imparted to them. These Kingdom principles were simple to take home and use in their spheres of influence. Living these principles for over 37 years as a Fortune 100 manager and trainer has produced great favor and influence for me to share my faith with others. It opened doors of opportunity that would have remained closed if they were not operating in my life. Once you step into these principles, God will lead you to minister to people you never imagined you would be able to before! Kingdom principles do one main thing—they allow us to reveal Christ's love to people so they can have the chance to turn to Him.

PRINCIPLES ALWAYS WORK

I want to relate a personal story of how God redeemed me when operating in these principles through a difficult circumstance. I needed my spiritual covering to bring me through the hardships I have faced to remind me of the importance of sticking to God's ways to live.

> *Then said He unto the disciples, it is*
> *impossible but that offences will come.*
> LUKE 17:1A KJV

After spending many years with a major Fortune 100 company and receiving very favorable performance recaps, I hit a major distraction. There was a severe accident involving my son, and we had to take care of him as caregivers. During this time, this accident got me so focused

PRINCIPLES OF SONS

on him that it affected all other areas of my life. I realized that he took preeminence, but I had to stay focused to maintain my job and my other family relationships.

The company I was working for had a grading system as follows:

- 5.0—Best of Class
  Very few received this performance rating.
- 4.0—Above Standard
  Some were able to attain this.
- 3.0—Standard
  You are doing your job effectively. Most received this grade.
- 2.0—Below Standard
- 1.0—It gets ugly!

Under a previous manager, I had averaged 3 and 4 ratings in all 5 of my key areas of focus. Now, I was under a new manager with a personality very different from mine. Although our thought processes differed, he was one of the best managers I had seen, specifically in creating productive processes. That fall, while visiting my territory, he graded me very highly, and we worked well together that year. Six months later, in the company's headquarters, I received my final review for the previous year from him. He asked me what kind of year I had. I told him it was a great year compared to my peers, coming in second in volume achievement and number one in financial management, a major focus area of the company.

My manager's response was that even though it was a good year for me, he did not like the way I got my results, so my performance rating became three 3's and two 1's. He put me on 90 days probation, and I could be terminated if I failed to make necessary changes.

THE HEART OF A SON

This conversation was shocking because our last meeting six months earlier had been favorable. How should I proceed, and how should I respond? Was I going to dishonor him? Should I contact the Vice President of the company to complain? I could call Human Resources and report him. I could defend myself and show him to be in the wrong. Or I could use this crisis as an opportunity to shut up, remain focused, and honor this man instead. Would I allow God to redeem me? This Scripture came to me:

> *But no weapon that is formed against you shall prosper, and every tongue that shall rise against you in judgment you shall show to be in the wrong. This [peace, righteousness, security, triumph over opposition] is the heritage of the servants of the Lord [those in whom the ideal Servant of the Lord is reproduced]; this is the righteousness or the vindication which they obtain from Me [this is that which I impart to them as their justification], says the Lord.*
> ISAIAH 54:17 AMPC

I kept hearing God's small, still voice saying, "Let Me defend you." I received spiritual counsel from my covering, decided not to defend myself to upper management, and to remain focused! I began to stand in faith on this Scripture every day and lifted my expectation up that God would make it right!

I had to get to work spiritually by standing on God's Word and naturally by WORKING on my assignments. I had to take personal responsibility. For the next 90 days, I refocused on my processes and areas that needed improvement. I provided weekly updates and outlined the follow-through in areas where he felt I needed to change. I showed an increase in the areas where I was graded poorly on in the performance evaluation. Every recap I put together and turned in, I did so with excellence.

I found accountability from a former co-worker who was promoted to my new boss. He flat out thought that I would be terminated after the 90 days, but he was there to oversee my reports and efforts. Many of us could use more accountability in our lives; it encourages solid progress and keeps you accountable to the principles necessary for your growth. I stayed in order under my boss and did not defend myself and complain about him to anyone else. I kept focused with the expectation that God would redeem me by meeting weekly with my spiritual covering for encouragement.

After monitoring me for six weeks, my boss's conclusion was that I just needed to make a few minor adjustments. He reported back to my manager to adjust both 1 score ratings back to 3. After much effort and consistency in those 90 days, my focus on these principles produced a major turnaround in my job. I served both my boss and my manager by following through on what they had asked. I showed my commitment to the company's success through my willingness to make the necessary changes.

After 90 days, I expected these principles to produce the necessary changes they demanded. I honored the people over myself, completed my work in excellence, and took personal responsibility. The next assessment I was going to hear from my manager was, "Great job!" For the rest of the year, while I managed my team, I did not hold a grudge toward my manager. Emphasizing his gifting and strengths, I

> I HONORED THE PEOPLE OVER MYSELF, COMPLETED MY WORK IN EXCELLENCE, AND TOOK PERSONAL RESPONSIBILITY

THE HEART OF A SON

began to serve his vision for the region. Consequently, I also began to see my results improve to levels I had never experienced before. You see, I was walking in these six powerful principles, and they produced great results in my personal and professional life. God used this experience to test these principles in my life. Without this test, I wouldn't have had the chance to grow from implementing them.

In Las Vegas that following March, I was in the National Sales Meeting, where they announced the recipient of the Sales Manager of the Year award. Who do you think they called to the stage? That's right, my name echoed in the room, and I was honored, along with my food broker, as the Manager and Broker of the Year! How could that be when I was on probation for three months with low ratings? God turned it all around as I obeyed His guidance in the process and practiced His Kingdom principles in this challenge. I became a Hero—I operated in all six of those powerful principles, and God redeemed me! Because I was covered in this day of battle as a son, I received the greater reward. These principles have come directly from my spiritual father and his teachings.

> *O God the Lord, the strength of my salvation, thou*
> *hast covered my head in the day of battle.*
> PSALM 140:7 KJV

By wisdom, I remained focused until a certain reward became evident in front of my own eyes. That manager and I continued in a good relationship until I retired. He moved on to new ventures with the company with success. He had a way of getting things done differently, and I needed to focus my execution on his way of doing things. By doing so, I received a great outcome – standing on a platform in front of hundreds of my peers as the Sales Manager of the Year!

PRINCIPLES OF SONS

Relating this idea to your heart as a son, take the time to watch your spiritual father's fruit from how he ministers to others. What principles is he living and teaching? Sons learn best from their fathers. Implement the following to develop your sonship:

Listen to the testimonies of those who interact with your spiritual father and be encouraged that, as his spiritual son, God will use you in a similar fashion. You, too, will minister wherever God has planted you when you live your life according to Kingdom principles.

Study the parables of Jesus to learn principles about being presence-driven and completely sold out for Christ and His Kingdom. These parables about the Kingdom of God will stir you up to learn more about being a son.

Proverbs and Matthew 5, 6, and 7 are also critical studies that reveal Kingdom patterns we should practice.

If your spiritual father has teachings on the Kingdom of God, purchase them and invest in studying these messages. They will launch you into new places for your journey. The Spirit of God will work in you and through you to bless others in new and exciting ways.

There are additional principles that we need to operate in the Kingdom to develop our character in the nature of Christ so we can reveal Him to the world.

1. **Purity and Holiness**: Live uprightly and walk in righteousness. The Kingdom of God is righteousness, peace, and joy. Notice the order of righteousness first.

    Follow peace with all men, and holiness,
    without which no man shall see the Lord.
    HEBREWS 11:14 KJV

THE HEART OF A SON

> *But I say, walk and live [habitually] in the [Holy] Spirit [responsive to and controlled and guided by the Spirit]; then you will certainly not gratify the cravings and desires of the flesh (of human nature without God).*
> GALATIANS 5:16 AMPC

2. **Praise and Worship**: I am a praiser, and in our church we have intense praise and worship. We get God's attention by creating an atmosphere for Him to move. Our church's motto is "Where Church Comes Alive!" We also always declare that we praise Him two times: when we feel like it and when we don't! In this time, you cannot afford to lose your praise. KEEP YOUR PRAISE ON! I am a worshipping warrior and was a worship leader for years, and I am free in my worship! Our church is known for its governmental praise and worship, and our flag/dance team can change atmospheres through their powerful and heartfelt expressions of praise. Everyone can praise God at any time and see His presence change the atmosphere around them.

> *But thou art holy, O thou that inhabitest the praises of Israel."*
> PSALMS 22:3 KJV

3. **Prayer and Intercession**: In our church, we have a prayer conference call on Monday – Friday mornings that includes a teaching from our apostle and prayer for our city and other needs. We have prayer on Tuesday nights and before Sunday and Wednesday services. Our prayer warriors have stopped a radical terrorist group from invading our city; these terrorists left because of prayer. They are in over 50 cities in the United States, and one of their own told us that our city was the only

city that they could not enter! We eliminated three psychic centers through prayer. We know how to pray from the heavens and bring answers to the earth through prophetic decrees and declarations.

Thou shalt also decree a thing, and it shall be established unto thee: and the light shall shine upon thy ways.
JOB 22:28 KJV

PRACTICAL FOCUS FOR PRINCIPLES

If you are going to operate in the Kingdom, then you need to do the following:

1. Have an anointed prayer life and know how to pray from the heavens. Study the prayer Jesus taught sons to say from Matthew 6:9-13.

    - What will you implement differently during your prayer time?

2. Live a life in the Spirit and do not fulfill the lust of your flesh (selfish nature). Overcome your soul realm and live in the Spirit by putting on the nature of God's image (Ephesians 4:19-24) in true righteousness and holiness by being responsive, guided, and directed by the Holy Spirit.

    - What are some things you need to cut out of your life so that you can live more of a Spirit-led life?

THE HEART OF A SON

3. You can praise your way through every battle as Israel always sent Judah first. You must be a worshipping warrior to operate in the Kingdom. Spend time each day praising God with and without music when you feel like it and when you don't.

    - What are the results of implementing consistent times of praise from a loving heart to your Heavenly Father?

4. Walk and live by the HEROES principles and see God's favor and influence come into your life, giving you the advantage in your personal and professional experiences.

    - Which of the HEROES principles can you live more in today?

    - Which ones are you already demonstrating in your life?

CHAPTER TEN
PROTOCOL OF SONS

There is protocol in the apostolic church required when serving under a spiritual father and mother. Protocol is defined as a system of rules that explain the correct conduct and procedures to be followed in formal situations. When I worked for the Coca-Cola Company, every year I had to read and sign the company's code of conduct document. I could not be in violation of this code, or I would be reprimanded or terminated. This kind of accountability is sadly lacking in churches today. This is where it should begin and be modeled for the world to follow!

By now, you are familiar that the apostolic church teaches and emphasizes sonship; we are sons of God!

> *Behold, what manner of love the Father hath bestowed upon us, that we should be called the sons of God: therefore the world knoweth us not, because it knew Him not.*
> 1 JOHN 3:1 KJV

So, as a son, operating in your church under your set man and woman of God, it is imperative to follow the protocol. This is the culture that is established or the apostolic code of conduct that they set forth. Here is what we have set in place in our church to give you an example:

- **Making Covenant**—The key to a longstanding relationship is a covenant. You must establish and live in a covenant relationship both vertically to God and horizontally to each other. Our first focus is advancing the Kingdom together! When you are rallied around such a cause, you will stick together to see it through to completion.

    And he said, Behold, I make a covenant: before all thy people I will do marvels, such as have not been done in all the earth, nor in any nation: and all the people among which thou art shall see the work of the Lord: for it is a terrible (awesome) thing that I will do with thee.
    EXODUS 34:10 KJV

- **Pioneering**—The apostolic cannot rely on a blueprint because we have never come this way before. Therefore, we need to come up and into His presence every day to be led by the Holy Spirit as we pioneer this path.

    After this I looked, and, behold, a door was opened in heaven: and the first voice which I heard was as it were of a trumpet talking with me; which said, Come up hither, and I will shew thee things which must be hereafter.
    REVELATION 4:1 KJV

- **Challenged to Change**—Your spiritual father's role is to make you uncomfortable to birth change in your life! Most people dislike change and remain in a place of maintaining what they

PROTOCOL OF SONS

know and where it is comfortable. Yet, change is necessary for true and accelerated growth.

You must prove your repentance by a changed life.
MATTHEW 3:8 TPT

- **Covering**—This area is most important to understand as an apostolic person under headship. A denomination cannot cover you—only a set man or woman has that authority. The protection for you and your family is found under this covering for your safety. Ones who lack covering in this hour are opening themselves to major battles that they do not have to fight alone if they stay covered. That's not to say you will not go through difficulty, but you will go through it more swiftly and more victoriously with your spiritual covering blanketing you. Furthermore, watch God use your difficulties to your advantage when you are properly covered.

> WITH YOUR SPIRITUAL COVERING BLANKETING YOU, YOU WILL GO THROUGH BATTLES MORE SWIFTLY AND VICTORIOUSLY

O God the Lord, the strength of my salvation, Thou hast covered my head in the day of battle.
PSALMS 140:7 KJV

- **Character**—To overcome the principalities and powers of evil in a region, you must operate in a spirit of holiness and righteousness. In the apostolic, your character will be tested and purged (the act of removing by cleansing, sanctify, remove the impurities). We are moving from gifting (outer court) to anointing (Holy Place) to character (Most Holy Place). It's time to be cleaned up and be filled up by the Spirit! Stay on the Highway of Holiness!

> *And a highway shall be there, and a way, and it shall be called The way of holiness; the unclean shall not pass over it; but it shall be for those: the wayfaring men, though fools, shall not err therein. No lion shall be there, nor any ravenous beast shall go up thereon, it shall not be found there; but the redeemed shall walk there: And the ransomed of the Lord shall return, and come to Zion with songs and everlasting joy upon their heads: they shall obtain joy and gladness, and sorrow and sighing shall flee away.*
>
> ISAIAH 35:8-10 KJV

- **Culture**—Each apostolic church has its own culture – based on honor, excellence, and servanthood. Remember to serve the set man, not the organization or denomination. The government is on the shoulders (you and me) and not on the head (set man). As a leader under the set man and woman, I must allow them to stay in God's presence. Our jobs are to pray, intercede, and do the work of the ministry. Moses was rebuked by his father-in-law for trying to manage all of the Israelites' disputes, and Jethro encouraged him to raise up leaders to take the responsibility of the people. We see this protocol again in Acts.

> *And in those days, when the number of the disciples was multiplied, there arose a murmuring of the Grecians*

against the Hebrews, because their widows were neglected in the daily ministration. Then the twelve called the multitude of the disciples unto them, and said, It is not reason that we should leave the Word of God, and serve tables. Wherefore, brethren, look ye out among you seven men of honest report, full of the Holy Ghost and wisdom, whom we may appoint over this business.
ACTS 6:1-3 KJV

- **Correction**—Based on the person, not on the issue, everyone will be corrected differently in an apostolic church, which many find difficult to swallow, especially rule-followers. Since people are at different maturity levels, the correction will be different for each. To much is given, much is required. Some are younger in the faith and need to be nurtured in the process. Others who are more mature and can receive the correction needed to make changes.

- **Capacity**—It is the maximum amount that something can contain, the amount that something can produce, or a specified role or position. In the apostolic, as you begin to change, you increase your capacity through more responsibility. Many times, to expand our capacity, we need to invest in ourselves by meditating on the messages from our set man/woman. You can also take an online or in-person course to improve your skill set. Put away the phone, turn off the TV, and read a book that edifies and expands learning in the Kingdom or your field of interest. Always be in a state of mind that is willing to be taught and to increase in new ways. Your personal university begins each evening from 6 to 11 PM and on weekends, so invest your time wisely.

THE HEART OF A SON

- **Cost**—To be a son in the Kingdom, will cost you everything—the apostolic message is to kill your selfish nature! Many people cannot handle an apostolic church because it forces them to change. Challenged by the Word, people become uncomfortable until they either shift or leave. I have seen people come into Jubilee Ministries and love what God is doing but refuse to change. They end up leaving to return to a lower lifestyle. Many say God told them to leave, but they never got any counsel. They will end up living at a lower 30-fold level. Had they changed when given the opportunity, they would have walked out the fullness of their assignment and destiny!

- **Protect the Anointing**—We must guard the anointing in the apostolic house of God and not become familiar with the set man or woman or the way they do things. Many times, new people come into the church and tell the apostle that they know best from their experiences and request him to change methods. We are in new territory as pioneers in the apostolic, so don't bring your old wineskin into the Father-Son Kingdom Age, the new realm where we are ascending. Those former ideas won't work! As you move into the apostolic, join in and embrace the culture and protocol that have been established by the set man. This is where you make a choice: either receive a greater anointing or get offended. Those who harbor an offense go back to the old wineskin (Egypt) and do not enter their Promised Land. Choose well!

- **Vision**—The apostolic vision is a corporate vision and is for the plurality of ministry. Apostolic ministries work in teams. However, we must understand the vision, how our gifting fits into it, and commit to accomplishing the vision. One vision, one voice, and one corporate man. This is our creed.

PROTOCOL OF SONS

- **Pursue Your Father**—He is not pursuing you; he is pursuing God! We are not in a pastoral paradigm where we meet weekly for coffee with the apostle. Our apostle has a huge assignment in taking cities and territories. These are great responsibilities, and apostles carry a heavy weight of glory to advance God's Kingdom within a people. We have a pastoral care team and elders who tend the sheep. He provides time to access him and his wife after services and in our weekly Café. Opportunities for growth come in a variety of ways: weekly services, conferences, outreach, prayer meetings, and more. In case of issues that cannot be answered by the elder or pastoral team, the apostle will give his input and become involved as needed. This is the Jethro principle in action. Read Exodus 18 and Acts 6:1-7 for a more detailed study.

- **Team Ministry**—If one fails on a team, we all fail. One for all and all for one. This might be hard for some, especially if you are doing all the right things. However, we are a team, and we need to be there to lift others up if they fail and provide support to make the ministry successful. Work with others who are different from you and learn to ebb and flow together, keeping the unity of the family of God.

- **Upgrades**—What you did this past year was good, but every year you must look to upgrade your responsibilities to advance the Kingdom in your local church. Maintain a journal of key learnings of what worked and what didn't work so you can improve. Daniel and the three Hebrew boys were rated at a 10 in all they did. What level are you? You can only bring others up to your level. If you are a 5, you can only take a person who is a 1, 2, 3, or 4 and bring them to your level. How can you upgrade to advance the Kingdom? Upgrades apply spiritually and naturally.

THE HEART OF A SON

- **Second Witness**—There must be a second witness to the preached word, prophetic word, worship, and prayer by making a statement of agreement. For example, you can verbally agree and stand up in church to agree with a preached word or prophetic word that is given. People are watching your response as a son. Sons lead in these examples and support their fathers.

- **Over-Communicate**—Communication and response go together. For every word put out by your spiritual father, there must be an active, quick, and detailed response—email, text, social media, or in person. Your voice must be heard! If you are in a position at your local church, you must always communicate to your spiritual leader to submit your ideas before you implement them. In fact, we call it over-communicating!

- **Servanthood**—You must be a servant. Be hands-on and do not wait to be told what to do when the requests are known and put out to you. Be proactive and complete needs before they are asked. You must know the heart of your set man and woman of God without them asking. Most apostles are very proactive and direct in getting things done.

- **Eliminate Strife**—As a leader and son, you must not allow any strife or murmuring to come forth from people in the congregation. Your job is to stop that immediately. If another leader is saying things against your set man/woman, this must be immediately communicated to the set man. Stop complaining and teach those who do so a better way by pointing to the Word of God and His promises. Encourage others to fast from negative words and to speak God's words of life in every circumstance. Personalities are subject to the nature of Christ. Allow Him to use you to promote harmony with your brothers and sisters in Christ.

PROTOCOL OF SONS

Do not allow strife to come between those in the family of God, and particularly against headship.

- **Prayed Up and Praise Ready**—Before you come into church, you must leave all your excess baggage outside, be praised up and prayed up to worship, have a joyful look on your face! Smile! From the first drum beat or strum of the guitar, express your praise and worship. We are privileged to be in God's house together. Be ready to minister to others at services and events. Come with both hands full, ready to pour out to God and into others! Do not come in with your hands empty by neglecting your own personal time with God.

> BE READY TO MINISTER TO GOD AND TO OTHERS

- **Prophetic Actions**—When the apostle tells you during the message to high five or tell your neighbor a phrase/word – do it! Follow through on prophetic acts. For example, we have gotten our keys out during a message and have shaken them around when our apostle taught on the keys of the Kingdom. We have also put out a red blanket or scarf over our door frames to represent the reality of Passover in our lives. A final example is during ministry time. Our apostle will ask us to do something we haven't done before after receiving prayer for healing. Many people receive their healing in full when they act on this request. Many of the Old Testament prophets used these prophetic actions to demonstrate the Word from God. The Gospels show Jesus demonstrating the prophetic in this way as well.

- **Anointed to Finish**—You have God's divine ability (grace) to finish strong! Any excuse is a lack of desire. Don't quit or give in. Your faith is measured by what can stop you. God sees the end from the beginning, and He will allow you to finish what He has begun.

- **Be a God lover of His presence!**—This is the most vital element of our church. Without God and His presence, we are nothing. One of the key messages of our ministry is The Presence Driven Life. Never forsake time with Him every day.

The lovers of God who chase after righteousness will find all their dreams come true: an abundant life drenched with favor and a fountain that overflows with satisfaction.
PROVERBS 21:21 TPT

PRACTICAL FOCUS FOR PROTOCOL

1. Protocols are important for any system to operate well.

    - What protocols have you seen work well in your life?

    - How do they align with Biblical protocols?

2. Review your experience with your set ministry.

    - What protocols from your spiritual father/mother have you struggled with, and which ones have you quickly employed?

PROTOCOL OF SONS

3. The apostolic church functions differently from a pastoral paradigm.

    - What are your experiences with both?

    - Share testimonies from apostolic protocols being activated in your life.

THE HEART OF A SON

PROTOCOL IS JUST A
CODE OF CONDUCT THAT
ENSURES ORDER AND
PROVIDES PROTECTION.

SUMMARY
POSITIVE IMPACT OF SONS

> *"For behold, the days are coming," says the Lord, "that I will bring back from captivity My people Israel and Judah," says the Lord. "And I will cause them to return to the land that I gave to their fathers, and they shall possess it."*
> JEREMIAH 30:3 NKJV

The apostolic is here to change generations so that they can positively impact and influence culture. We are in a cultural war right now, and we need to educate, equip, and empower this generation to become a military might to identify their assignments, achieve their purposes, and fulfill their destinies. This is the call of the apostles and their sons in this day and hour.

It's time to build this generation by helping them master the Kingdom principles and come into maturity at a young age. I thank God for our young people who know their assignments, but as a wall-less church, we must take this truth out into our community and see the change!

Our first area of focus as a son is to be transformed and conformed to the image and likeness of His Son, Jesus. This is the key—to be a true son in these days of the Kingdom of God advancing in the earth is our highest calling.

THE HEART OF A SON

I received this prophetic word recently, and I pray that it will bless you to think as a wall-less ministry and outside of the box of your experiences.

Father, I just impart to my brother a capacity to be outside the frame of reference that he is already aware of. He has gained knowledge, he has gained experience, and those things that have formed constants, but there is something outside of the box, literally outside the box. That which has not been seen, that which there is no frame of reference for. This is that place of inventive concepts that come seemingly out of nowhere.

So I just release to my brother in his mind, in his spirit, and in that place of creation, the ability to step out of the frames of reference, to see what's never been seen before, to think and receive from You revelation that his natural mind has never even conceived of. Lord, they are things that are revelation beyond points of reference of his current experience and reality, Lord Jesus, and it's exactly what you want to give to him in that place in Jesus' name.

POSITIVE IMPACT OF SONS

PRACTICAL FOCUS FOR MAKING A POSTIVE IMPACT

I believe this is what the Lord is speaking to sons today through this word. Journal your reflections on these thoughts.

1. For us to have the heart of a son, we need to increase our capacity for the Kingdom. Capacity is the amount that can be contained, the power to learn or retain knowledge.

    - What are you doing now to increase your capacity in your gifting and anointing?

    - What are you doing to build your character?

    - What online classes, books, and other areas are you focused on upgrading this year?

2. We need to change our frame of reference (our set of ideas, conditions, or assumptions that determine how something will be approached, perceived, or understood). God brings us through our personal difficulties and experiences to mature us as believers.

    - What is your frame of reference you are operating in consistently? It must not be the worldly frame of reference but must be a revelation of the Kingdom of God and how to operate in it.

- How are you going to change your frame of reference to be Kingdom-minded?

3. Are you operating in the HEROES principles of Honor, Excellence, Responsibility, Order, Expectation, and Servanthood? Do you have the passion to forget the past and look to the future to the victory prize of seeing the Kingdom of God established in the earth?

- Rewrite the story—your present and future—without the sorrow of the past.

CONCLUSION

The Apostle Paul sums things up this way:

> *My passion is to be consumed with him and not cling to my own "righteousness" based in keeping the written Law. My only "righteousness" will be His, based on the faithfulness of Jesus Christ—the very righteousness that comes from God. And I continually long to know the wonders of Jesus and to experience the overflowing power of His resurrection working in me. I will be one with Him in His sufferings and become like Him in His death. Only then will I be able to experience complete oneness with Him in His resurrection from the realm of death.*

POSITIVE IMPACT OF SONS

I admit that I haven't yet acquired the absolute fullness that I'm pursuing, but I run with passion into his abundance so that I may reach the purpose for which Christ Jesus laid hold of me to make me His own. I don't depend on my own strength to accomplish this; however, I do have one compelling focus: I forget all of the past as I fasten my heart to the future instead.

I run straight for the divine invitation of reaching the heavenly goal and gaining the victory-prize through the anointing of Jesus. So let all who are fully mature have this same passion, and if anyone is not yet gripped by these desires, God will reveal it to them. And let us all advance together to reach this victory-prize, following one path with one passion.
PHILIPPIANS 3:9-16 TPT

The heart of a true son is:

- to become mature by your passion,
- to attain the high calling of God,
- to be transformed and conformed into His image and likeness,
- and to advance His Kingdom in the planet by serving the corporate vision under the set man or woman of God.

Enjoy the journey and just BE HIS SON!

THE HEART OF A SON

YOUR FOCUS DETERMINES YOUR FUTURE.

APPENDIX

Below is our church's mandate to inspire you as a son of God!

JUBILEE MINISTRIES INTERNATIONAL CITY CHURCH MANDATE

Jubilee Ministries is an apostolic and prophetic church. As prophetic people, we have an understanding of the times. As an apostolic people, we are change agents sent to influence and change our world.

We are God's holy nation, a chosen generation, a royal priesthood, and treasured people. We are Evangelical, winning souls for the Kingdom of God. We are Pentecostal, a Holy Ghost community filled with God's supernatural power, created for signs and wonders. We are Kingdom—a military might invading the seven mountains of society, transforming culture, and filling our world with the Glory of God.

We are Kings and Priests unto our God. As Priests, we have compassion for mankind, and as Kings, we have the authority to transform their lives. As Priests, we are worshipers, and as Kings, we are warriors. We are chosen for greatness, and together we shall do great exploits! Our individual destinies are found in our corporate identity.

As the Tabernacle of David, we are a people without prejudice and a people of praise; we take vengeance over all our enemies and rule over every circumstance!

We are the seed of Abraham and the seed of David. As the seed of Abraham, we are promised the land, and as the seed of David, we are promised the throne. The land is the earth, and the throne is our legal right to rule it.

We are chosen for greatness and anointed to finish. Nothing shall deter us from enforcing the finished work of Calvary in our world! We have come to the Kingdom for such a time as this! We have come together to make Jesus, King and Lord over all the earth. Our purpose is to be intimate with the Lord, and our destiny is to manifest Him in the earth! We are the voice of Jubilee to our generation. Jubilee Ministries International is a place where dreams come true!

APPENDIX

MEET THE AUTHOR

Ed Turose is an expert Focus Strategist who is skilled in planning the best way for you and your organization to gain an advantage and achieve greater levels of success and performance. Ed has over 40 years of leadership and business experience as a people manager, trainer, consultant, and strategic planner for two Fortune 100 companies, Unilever, as a manager for ten years and twenty-seven years with The Coca-Cola Company before becoming the President of the Focus Life Institute.

He is known as "The Focus Coach" and has authored books, educational development tools, and marketplace resources. The cause of The Focus Life Institute is to educate, equip, and empower individuals to focus on identifying their personal calling and assignment in life, achieving their purpose, and fulfilling their destiny!

Ed Turose Experience

- President of Focus Life Institute, LLC
- Focusize™ Strategist, Focus Coach, Consultant, Trainer, and Motivational Speaker
- Doctorate of Divinity from Tabernacle Bible College, Tampa, Florida, 2013
- Senior National Account Manager and Trainer for The Coca-Cola Company (27 years)
- Regional Sales Manager, Unilever (10 years)
- Consultant and CEO of Victory Corporate Consulting 1995 - 2015
- Adjunct Business Professor, Geneva College, Beaver Falls, PA

THE HEART OF A SON

- Certified Trainer
- DiSC Behavioral System (1992)
- Ken Blanchard's Situational Leadership
- Think Inc. Negotiation
- Karrass Negotiation
- Author of *The Focused Fulfilled Life, The HEROES Effect, The HEROES Principles, Be a Hero,* and *The Heart of a Son*
- *Focusize™* Podcasts and internet *Focus Life* TV Show
- Creator of F.A.S.T. (Focused Advanced Skills Training) Online Business Courses, Your Unique Assessment, 40 Days of Focus, and additional business courses
- Developer and creator of the Career and Workplace Preparation Educational Courses for Grades K-12, colleges, universities, and reentry programs www.focuslifeinstitute.com
- President of the Christian Chamber of Commerce of Pennsylvania
- Member of USCAL (United States Coalition of Apostolic Leaders)
- Chief Administrative officer of Global Impact Mega Corporation
- Member of (INK) International Network of Kingdom Leaders

For speaking or training opportunities, contact
eturose@focuslifeintitute.com

To learn more:

www.focuslifeinstitute.com

www.edturose.com

APPENDIX

CONTINUE YOUR FOCUS PROGRESSION WITH OUR ONLINE COURSES

The HEROES Principles help individuals identify what specific virtues they need to improve on to be effective in school, church, or the workplace. Included are practical applications for each virtue and personal stories. Applying these virtues will produce favor and increase opportunities for influence and advancement within your personal and professional life.

H - HONOR

E - EXCELLENCE

R - RESPONSIBILITY

O - ORDER

E - EXPECTATION

S - SERVANTHOOD

How To Find Life's Direction was designed to help prepare you for your future! This e-course will provide you with a process to focus on your career path and be prepared for your future. The e-Course is an all-inclusive practical development tool based on your personal behavioral style. Sessions include Vision, Personality, Passion, Profession, and Peak Performance. Our online course includes personalized profiles, videos, PDFs, note-taking ability, exams, facilitator guides, and a course certificate.

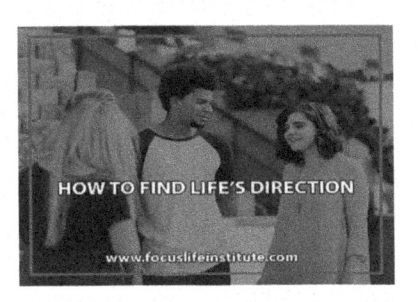

THE HEART OF A SON

Skills for Success was designed to help you improve your soft skills to gain greater levels of success. According to employers, graduates are not prepared for the workplace. Many companies have reported that graduates lack essential (soft) and critical thinking skills. Our Skills for Success Course offers skills training in communication, collaboration, conflict resolution, confidence, creativity, and character. In addition, we provide critical thinking skills for decision-making and problem-solving. We include time management and interviewing skills that produce greater levels of achievement and advancement within the workplace.

Focus on Entrepreneurship reviews the behavioral traits and characteristics of entrepreneurs. Recently, a great deal of focus has been on entrepreneurship and operating with an entrepreneurial spirit. The outcomes for this course are as follows:

- Gain an understanding of basic entrepreneurship
- Discover the qualities of successful entrepreneurs
- Comparing and contrasting entrepreneurship and traditional employment
- Uncover the personal characteristics of an entrepreneur
- Learn the specific behaviors of unstoppable entrepreneurs
- Be equipped with an understanding of self and the personality styles of others

APPENDIX

- Discover the entrepreneur characteristics of DISC Behavioral Styles
- Acquire the basic components of a business plan
- Gain insights for success for Innovation, Concepts, Execution, and Solutions
- Create a personal vision for your own business

ED TUROSE BOOKS

The Focus Fulfilled Life—People are consumed by an obsession to produce. This causes stress, anxiety, pressure, and oppression. God's plan allows for a natural rhythm of work and rest that is overflowing with faith and hope, free from stress, filled with provision, and designed for victory. In this book, *The Focus Fulfilled Life*, Ed shows you how to create a process for a lifestyle of focus by using the Word of God and activating your faith. A life of focus will produce a harvest of greater results. Experience the power of *The Focus Fulfilled Life* as you stand in faith and see a manifestation of the promises of God. Your journey to see greater results begins with the Focus Fulfilled Life Progression.

- Identify goals in your spiritual, emotional, physical, social, and financial life
- Gather and meditate on specific Scriptures related to these goals
- Develop daily strategies and capture your results
- Celebrate, rest, and testify of God's goodness and faithfulness

THE HEART OF A SON

The HEROES Principle—Statistics bear witness to the fact that trust and confidence have reached an all-time low. With our expectations of people near rock bottom, it is no wonder we have romanticized superheroes and lost ourselves in a world of fantasy. *The HEROES Principle* is comprised of six virtues all but lost to our society. They are Honor, Excellence, Responsibility, Order, Expectation, and Servanthood. Imagine the favor and blessing that would come to you if you began to incorporate these six powerful principles in your own life. Dr. Ed Turose describes these principles and provides application steps to equip you to put these principles into practice. *The HEROES Principle* will take you to a higher realm of living—more fulfilled and more engaged. Operating in these principles will allow you to reach your full potential and experience greater levels of success. By living these truths, you can begin to create a more positive environment around you and affect your sphere of influence. This is a faith-based book.

The HEROES Effect—Learn the six key virtues that will produce FAVOR, INCREASE & INFLUENCE in your life. Practical, powerful, and easy to put into practice, these six principles will catapult you to a new level of fulfillment and success. Step into a higher realm. Gain the edge and start leveraging your advantage as you create a more positive environment around you and attract the right people and opportunities into your life.

APPENDIX

BE A HERO—equip youth to influence their world! When you begin to apply the HEROES Principle, you will begin to experience favor in your life. Favor is the approval, support, popularity, or preference of a person or group. Favor makes you irresistible and attracts others to you. Favor takes you to the top of your sphere and makes you look good. When you see favor come into your life, then you begin to draw others to you, to be like you, hang around you and follow you. Favor puts you on the front line and helps you fulfill your destiny. It cannot be mediocre, ordinary, or second-rate. Favor is a powerful force that will bring important people to you. Favor will have people seek you out to invest in your dreams and ask how they can help you become even more successful. However, if you do not invest in yourself, work on improving your strengths, and practice these principles that you have learned. It's time for you to fulfill your assignment and begin to influence your sphere with these powerful principles that will encourage others but also bring fulfillment to you.

See all our online courses by visiting our website!

FOCUSLIFE INSTITUTE

www.focuslifeinstitute.com

THE HEART OF A SON

BECOME A FOCUS COACH

You can make a difference by becoming a certified Focus Coach by impacting this generation in multiple arenas—Education, Business, Recovery/Reentry. Whether you are a seasoned coach or want to begin a new career, the Focus Life development tools are an exciting addition to your coaching portfolio. Our passion is to change and impact this generation. We have a personalized program that brings hope to the hopeless and helps individuals focus on their own lens producing greater results. We believe our Focus Life courses will bring knowledge into your clients' lives that will produce personal experiences creating a greater quality of life for them now and in the future.

Please email **contact@focuslifeinstitute.com** for more details.